Second Workshop on Coreference Resolution Beyond OntoNotes (CORBON 2017)

Valencia, Spain
4 April 2017

ISBN: 978-1-5108-3863-5

Printed from e-media with permission by:

Curran Associates, Inc.
57 Morehouse Lane
Red Hook, NY 12571

Some format issues inherent in the e-media version may also appear in this print version.

Printed by Curran Associates, Inc. (2017)

For permission requests, please contact the Association for Computational Linguistics at the address below.

Association for Computational Linguistics
209 N. Eighth Street
Stroudsburg, Pennsylvania 18360

Phone: 1-570-476-8006
Fax: 1-570-476-0860

acl@aclweb.org

Additional copies of this publication are available from:

Curran Associates, Inc.
57 Morehouse Lane
Red Hook, NY 12571 USA
Phone: 845-758-0400
Fax: 845-758-2633
Email: curran@proceedings.com
Web: www.proceedings.com

Introduction

Many NLP researchers, especially those not working in the area of discourse processing, tend to equate coreference resolution with the sort of coreference that people did in MUC, ACE, and OntoNotes, having the impression that coreference is a well-worn task owing in part to the large number of papers reporting results on the MUC/ACE/OntoNotes corpora. This is an unfortunate misconception: the previous SemEval 2010 and CoNLL 2012 shared tasks on coreference resolution have largely focused on entity coreference, which constitutes only one of the many kinds of coreference relations that were discussed in theoretical and computational linguistics in the past few decades. In fact, by focusing on entity coreference resolution, NLP researchers have only scratched the surface of the wealth of interesting problems in coreference resolution.

The decision to focus on entity coreference resolution was initially made by information extraction (IE) researchers when coreference was selected as one of the tasks in the MUC-6 coreference in 1995. Many interesting kinds of coreference relations, such as bridging and reference to abstract entities, were left out not because they were not important, but because "it was felt that the menu was simply too ambitious". It turned out that this decision had an important consequence: the progress made in coreference research in the past two decades was largely driven by the availability of coreference-annotated corpora such as MUC, ACE, and OntoNotes, where entity coreference was the focus.

Being aware of other fora gathering coreference-related papers (such as LAW, DiscoMT or EVENTS), in 2016 we started a new workshop on the single topic of knowledge-oriented coreference resolution under the name of *Coreference Resolution Beyond OntoNotes* (CORBON) that would bring together researchers who were interested in under-investigated coreference phenomena, willing to contribute both theoretical and applied computational work on coreference resolution, especially for languages other than English, less-researched forms of coreference and new applications of coreference resolution.

The success of the first edition of the workshop (held in conjunction with NAACL HLT 2016 in San Diego, USA) and our intention to verify the role of the Europe-based researchers in the field encouraged us to organise the second edition of the workshop in conjunction with EACL 2017 in Valencia, Spain. Our call attracted 12 submissions (nine from European research institutions and three from India). We are pleased to see that the submissions covered not only a variety of less-studied languages in the coreference community (e.g., Basque, French, German, Polish, Portuguese, Russian, and Tamil) but also many under-investigated topics in coreference resolution (e.g., feature representation, the use of semantics and deep syntax for coreference resolution, difficult cases of anaphora, and the use of coreference chains in high-level natural language applications). Each submission was rigorously reviewed by three to five programme committee members. We would like to thank the 29 programme committee members for their hard work. Based on their recommendations, we accepted six papers.

We are grateful to Massimo Poesio for accepting our invitation to be this year's invited speaker. Massimo will give us an overview of his new project on developing better games and techniques to collect and analyse data about anaphora and using them to train probabilistic resolvers.

To further enrich the workshop participants' experience, we included in this year's programme a panel discussion on the interplay of referential and discourse relations in text. We thank Ruslan Mitkov, Anna Nedoluzhko, Massimo Poesio, and Arndt Riester for agreeing to serve as panelists. We are excited about this new addition to the programme.

To promote work on coreference resolution in low-resource languages, we included in our call for papers a shared task on projection-based coreference resolution. The goal was to perform German and Russian coreference resolution by projecting automatically generated coreference chains from English to these languages via a parallel corpus. In particular, the participants were not allowed to employ any knowledge of these languages or use any German and Russian coreference-annotated data to train resolvers in these languages. To our knowledge, this is the first shared task on projection-based coreference resolution. We are indebted to our shared task coordinator, Yulia Grishina, who capably handled all aspects of the shared task, ranging from data preparation to the scoring of the participating systems. Papers related to the shared task, including Yulia's overview paper and the participating team's system description paper, are included in the proceedings and will be presented during the workshop.

Finally, we would like to thank the workshop participants for joining in. We look forward to an exciting workshop in Valencia.

— Maciej Ogrodniczuk and Vincent Ng

Organizing Committee and Proceedings Editors:

Maciej Ogrodniczuk, Institute of Computer Science, Polish Academy of Sciences
Vincent Ng, University of Texas at Dallas

Shared Task Coordinator:

Yulia Grishina, University of Potsdam

Programme Committee:

Anders Björkelund, University of Stuttgart
Antonio Branco, University of Lisbon
Chen Chen, Google
Dan Cristea, A. I. Cuza University of Iaşi
Pascal Denis, MAGNET, INRIA Lille Nord-Europe
Sobha Lalitha Devi, AU-KBC Research Center, Anna University, Chennai
Yulia Grishina, University of Potsdam
Lars Hellan, Norwegian University of Science and Technology
Veronique Hoste, Ghent University
Yufang Hou, IBM
Ryu Iida, National Institute of Information and Communications Technology (NICT)
Ekaterina Lapshinova-Koltunski, Saarland University
Emmanuel Lassalle, Citadel, UK
Chen Li, Microsoft
Sebastian Martschat, Heidelberg University
Ruslan Mitkov, University of Wolverhampton
Costanza Navarretta, University of Copenhagen
Anna Nedoluzhko, Charles University in Prague
Michal Novak, Charles University in Prague
Maciej Ogrodniczuk, Institute of Computer Science, Polish Academy of Sciences
Constantin Orasan, University of Wolverhampton
Massimo Poesio, University of Essex
Manfred Stede, University of Potsdam
Veselin Stoyanov, Facebook
Yannick Versley, Heidelberg University
Rob Voigt, Stanford University
Sam Wiseman, Harvard University
Amir Zeldes, Georgetown University
Heike Zinsmeister, University of Hamburg

Invited Speaker:

Massimo Poesio, University of Essex

Panelists:

Ruslan Mitkov, University of Wolverhampton
Anna Nedoluzhko, Charles University in Prague
Massimo Poesio, University of Essex
Arndt Riester, University of Stuttgart

Table of Contents

Use Generalized Representations, But Do Not Forget Surface Features
Nafise Sadat Moosavi and Michael Strube 1

Enriching Basque Coreference Resolution System using Semantic Knowledge sources
Ander Soraluze, Olatz Arregi, Xabier Arregi and Arantza Díaz de Ilarraza 8

Improving Polish Mention Detection with Valency Dictionary
Maciej Ogrodniczuk and Bartłomiej Nitoń 17

A Google-Proof Collection of French Winograd Schemas
Pascal Amsili and Olga Seminck 24

Using Coreference Links to Improve Spanish-to-English Machine Translation
Lesly Miculicich Werlen and Andrei Popescu-Belis 30

Multi-source annotation projection of coreference chains: assessing strategies and testing opportunities
Yulia Grishina and Manfred Stede 41

CORBON 2017 Shared Task: Projection-Based Coreference Resolution
Yulia Grishina 51

Projection-based Coreference Resolution Using Deep Syntax
Michal Novák, Anna Nedoluzhko and Zdeněk Žabokrtský 56

Workshop Program: April 4, 2017

09:30–11:00	**Session 1: Invited Talk, Feature Representations**
09:30–09:40	*Introduction* Maciej Ogrodniczuk and Vincent Ng
09:40–10:40	Invited talk: *Exploring Anaphoric Ambiguity Using Games-With-a-Purpose: The Dali Project* Massimo Poesio
10:40–11:00	*Use Generalized Representations, But Do Not Forget Surface Features* Nafise Sadat Moosavi, Michael Strube
11:00–11:30	**Coffee Break**
11:30–13:00	**Session 2: Coreference in Under-Investigated Languages**
11:30–12:00	*Enriching Basque Coreference Resolution System using Semantic Knowledge Sources* Ander Soraluze, Olatz Arregi, Xabier Arregi, Arantza Díaz de Ilarraza
12:00–12:30	*Improving Polish Mention Detection with Valency Dictionary* Maciej Ogrodniczuk, Bartłomiej Nitoń
12:30–13:00	*A Google-Proof Collection of French Winograd Schemas* Pascal Amsili, Olga Seminck
13:00–14:30	**Lunch Break**
14:30–16:00	**Session 3: Panel Discussion, Coreference for NLP Applications**
14:30–15:30	Panel discussion: *Referential vs. discourse relations* Ruslan Mitkov, Anna Nedoluzhko, Massimo Poesio, Arndt Riester
15:30–16:00	*Using Coreference Links to Improve Spanish-to-English Machine Translation* Lesly Miculicich Werlen, Andrei Popescu-Belis
16:00–16:30	**Coffee Break**
16:30–18:00	**Session 4: Projection-Based Coreference Resolution**
16:30–17:00	*Multi-source Annotation Projection of Coreference Chains: Assessing Strategies and Testing Opportunities* Yulia Grishina, Manfred Stede
17:00–17:30	*CORBON 2017 Shared Task: Projection-Based Coreference Resolution* Yulia Grishina
17:30–18:00	*Projection-based Coreference Resolution Using Deep Syntax* Michal Novák, Anna Nedoluzhko, Zdeněk Žabokrtský

Use Generalized Representations, But Do Not Forget Surface Features

Nafise Sadat Moosavi and **Michael Strube**
Heidelberg Institute for Theoretical Studies gGmbH
Schloss-Wolfsbrunnenweg 35
69118 Heidelberg, Germany
{nafise.moosavi|michael.strube}@h-its.org

Abstract

Only a year ago, all state-of-the-art coreference resolvers were using an extensive amount of surface features. Recently, there was a paradigm shift towards using word embeddings and deep neural networks, where the use of surface features is very limited. In this paper, we show that a simple SVM model with surface features outperforms more complex neural models for detecting anaphoric mentions. Our analysis suggests that using generalized representations and surface features have different strength that should be both taken into account for improving coreference resolution.

1 Introduction

Coreference resolution is the task of finding different mentions that refer to the same entity in a given text. Anaphoricity detection is an important step for coreference resolution. An anaphoricity detection module discriminates mentions that are coreferent with one of the previous mentions. If a system recognizes mention m as non-anaphoric, it does not need to make any coreferent links for the pairs in which m is the anaphor.

The current state-of-the-art coreference resolvers (Wiseman et al., 2016; Clark and Manning, 2016a; Clark and Manning, 2016b), as well as their anaphoricity detection modules, use deep neural networks, word embeddings and a small set of features describing surface properties of mentions. While it is shown that this small set of features has significant impact on the overall performance (Clark and Manning, 2016a), their use is very limited in the state-of-the-art systems in comparison to the embedding features.

In this paper, we first introduce a new neural model for anaphoricity detection that considerably outperforms the anaphoricity detection of the state-of-the-art coreference resolver, i.e. deep-coref introduced by Clark and Manning (2016a). However, we show that a simple SVM model that is adapted from our coreferent mention detection approach (Moosavi and Strube, 2016), significantly outperforms the more complex neural models. We show that the SVM model also generalizes better than the neural model on a new domain other than the CoNLL dataset.

2 Discriminating Mentions for Coreference Resolution

The recognition of various categories of mentions can be beneficial for coreference resolution. The detection of the following categories is most common in the literature: (1) non-referential, (2) discourse-old, and (3) coreferent mentions. One can also discriminate other categories of mentions like mentions that are unlikely to be antecedents or discourse-new mentions (Uryupina, 2009). However, they are not common in comparison to the above categories.

2.1 Non-Referential Mentions

Non-referential mentions do not refer to an entity. These mentions only fill a syntactic position. For instance, "it" in "it is raining" is a non-referential mention. The approaches proposed by Evans (2001), Müller (2006), Bergsma et al. (2008), Bergsma and Yarowsky (2011) are examples of detecting non-referential cases of the pronoun *it*. Byron and Gegg-Harrison (2004) present a more general approach for detecting non-referential noun phrases.

Proceedings of the 2nd Workshop on Coreference Resolution Beyond OntoNotes (CORBON 2017), co-located with EACL 2017, pages 1–7,
Valencia, Spain, April 4, 2017.

2.2 Discourse-Old Mentions

Each mention can be assessed from the point of view of the discourse model (Prince, 1992). According to the discourse model, a mention may be new, old or inferable. Mentions which introduce a new entity into the discourse are *discourse-new* mentions. A discourse-new mention may be a singleton or it may be the first mention of a coreference chain. For instance, The first "Plato" in Example 2.1 is a *discourse-new* mention.

Example 2.1. *Plato* was a philosopher in Classical Greece. *This philosopher* is the founder of the Academy in Athens. *Plato* died at the age of 81.

A *discourse-old* mention refers to an entity that is already evoked in the discourse. Except for first mentions of coreference chains, other coreferent mentions are *discourse-old.* For instance, "this philosopher" and the second "Plato" in Example 2.1 are *discourse-old* mentions.

A mention is *inferable* if the hearer can infer the identity of the mention from another entity that has already been evoked in the discourse. "the windows" in Example 2.2 is an *inferable* mention.

Example 2.2. I walked into *the room. The windows* were all open.

The detection of discourse-old mentions is commonly referred to as *anaphoricity detection* (e.g. Zhou and Kong (2009), Ng (2009), Wiseman et al. (2015), Lassalle and Denis (2015), inter alia) while the task of anaphoric mention detection, based on its original definition, is of no use for coreference resolution. Mentions whose interpretations do not depend on previous mentions are called *non-anaphoric* mentions (van Deemter and Kibble, 2000). For example, both "Plato"s in Example 2.1 are non-anaphoric.

For consistency with the coreference literature, we refer to the task of discourse-old mention detection as anaphoricity detection.

Currently, all the state-of-the-art coreference resolvers learn anaphoricity detection jointly with coreference resolution (Wiseman et al., 2015; Wiseman et al., 2016; Clark and Manning, 2016a). The approaches proposed by Ng and Cardie (2002), Ng (2004), Ng (2009), Zhou and Kong (2009), Uryupina (2009) are examples of independent anaphoricity detection approaches.

2.3 Coreferent Mentions

Marneffe et al. (2015) discriminate mentions as coreferent vs. non-coreferent. Coreferent mentions are those mentions that appear in a coreference chain. A non-coreferent mention therefore can be a non-referential noun phrase or a referential noun phrase whose entity is only mentioned once (i.e. singleton). The proposed approaches of Recasens et al. (2013), Marneffe et al. (2015), and Moosavi and Strube (2016) discriminate mentions for coreference resolution this way.

3 Anaphoricity Detection Models

Anaphoricity detection is the most common approach for discriminating mentions for a coreference resolver. All of the state-of-the-art coreference resolvers use anaphoricity detection. In this paper, we compare three different anaphoricity detection approaches: two approaches using neural networks and word embeddings, and one using an SVM model and surface features. Clark and Manning (2016a) introduce the first neural model. Since Clark and Manning (2016a) train their anaphoricity model jointly with the coreference model, we refer to this model as the joint model. We introduce a new anaphoricity detection model as the second neural model using a Long-Short Term Memory (LSTM) network (Hochreiter and Schmidhuber, 1997). The third approach is adapted from our state-of-the-art coreferent mention detection (Moosavi and Strube, 2016).

3.1 Joint Model

As one of the neural models for anaphoricity detection, we consider the anaphoricity module of deep-coref[1], the state-of-the-art coreference resolution system introduced by Clark and Manning (2016a). This model has three layers for encoding different types of information regarding a mention. The first layer encodes the word embeddings of the head, first, last, two previous/following words, and the syntactic parent of the mention. The second layer encodes the averaged word embeddings of the five previous/following words, all words of the mention, sentence words, and document words. The third layer encodes the following features of a mention: type, length, position and whether it is embedded in another mention. The outputs of these three layers are combined into one vector and then get passed through a network with two hidden layers. This anaphoricity model is trained

[1]Available at `https://github.com/clarkkev/deep-coref`

jointly with the deep-coref coreference model.

3.2 LSTM Model

In this section we propose a new neural model for anaphoricity detection. Apart from the properties of the mention itself, we consider a limited number of surrounding words. We first generalize the context of a mention by removing the mention from the context and replacing it with a special placeholder. In our experiments, we consider the 10 previous and following words of a mention. We concatenate the mention tokens and the head token to the generalized word sequence. We separate the head and mention tokens in the concatenated sequence using two different placeholders.

The word embeddings of the above sequence are encoded using a bidirectional LSTM. LSTMs show convincing results on generating meaningful representations for various NLP tasks (e.g. Sutskever et al. (2014) and Vinyals et al. (2014)).

We also incorporate a set of surface features that contains (1) mention type (proper, nominal (definite, indefinite), pronouns (*he, I, it, she, they, we, you*)), (2) string match in the text, (3) string match in the previous context, (4) head match in the text, (5) head match in the previous context, (6) contains tokens of another mention, (7) contains tokens of a previous mention, (8) contained in another mention, (9) contained in a previous mention, and (10) embedded in another mention. These features are concatenated with the output of the bidirectional LSTM and get passed through one more layer that generates the output.

We also experiment with a more complex model including two different LSTMs for encoding mentions and their surrounding words. We consider longer sequences of previous words and an attention mechanism for processing the long sequence. However, the performance did not improve upon the LSTM model while it considerably increased the training time.

3.2.1 Implementation Details

Hyperparameters are tuned on the CoNLL 2012 development set. We minimize the cross entropy loss using gradient-based optimization and the Adam update rule (Kingma and Ba, 2014). We use minibatches of size 50. A dropout (Hinton et al., 2012) with a rate of 0.3 is applied to the output of LSTM. We initialize the embeddings with the 300-dimensional Glove embeddings (Pennington et al., 2014). The size of LSTM's hidden layer is set to 128. The model is trained in only one epoch.

3.3 SVM Model

Our SVM model introduced in Moosavi and Strube (2016), achieves state-of-the-art results for coreferent mention detection. This model uses the following set of features: lemmas and POS tags of all words of a mention, lemmas and POS tags of the two previous/following words, mention string, mention length, mention type (proper, nominal, pronoun, list), string match in the text, and head match in the text. We use a similar SVM model for anaphoricity detection. In addition to the features we used for coreferent mention detection, we also add the following features for anaphoricity detection: string match in the previous context, head match in the previous context, mention words are contained in another mention, mention words are contained in a previous mention, mention contains words of another mention, mention contains words of a previous mention. Similar to Moosavi and Strube (2016), we use an anchored SVM (Goldberg and Elhadad, 2007) with a polynomial kernel of degree two and remove feature-values that occur less than 10 times. The use of an anchored SVM with pruning helps the model to generalize better on new domains (Goldberg and Elhadad, 2009).

4 Performance Evaluation

We evaluate the anaphoricity models on the CoNLL 2012 dataset. It is worth noting that all of the examined anaphoricity detectors in this section use the same mention detection module and results are reported using system detected mentions. The performance of the mention detection module is of crucial importance for anaphoricity detection. Therefore, it is important that the compared anaphoricity detectors use the same mention detection.

	Non-Anaphoric			Anaphoric		
	R	P	F1	R	P	F1
joint	-	-	-	81.81	77.18	79.43
LSTM	90.71	92.64	91.66	85.00	81.48	83.20
LSTM*	90.51	87.31	88.88	72.64	78.64	75.52
SVM	92.42	92.61	92.51	84.66	84.30	84.48

Table 1: Results on the CoNLL 2012 test set.

The LSTM model that is described in Section 3.2 is denoted as *LSTM* in Table 1. In order to investigate the effect of the used surface features, we also report the results of the LSTM model without using these features (*LSTM**).

The following observations can be drawn from the results of Table 1: (1) our LSTM model outperforms the joint model while using less features and being trained independently, (2) the results of the LSTM* model is considerably lower than those of LSTM, especially for recognizing anaphoric mentions, and (3) the simple SVM model outperforms the neural models in detecting both anaphoric and non-anaphoric mentions.

4.1 Generalization Evaluation

In order to investigate the generalization on new domains, we evaluate the LSTM and SVM models on the WikiCoref dataset (Ghaddar and Langlais, 2016). The WikiCoref dataset is annotated according to the same annotation guideline as that of CoNLL. Therefore, it is an appropriate dataset for performing out-of-domain evaluations when CoNLL is used for training. For the experiments of Table 2, all models are trained on the CoNLL 2012 training data and tested on the WikiCoref dataset.

The word dictionary that is used for the LSTM model is built based on the CoNLL 2012 training data. All words that are not included in this dictionary are treated as out of vocabulary words with randomly initialized word embeddings. We further improve the performance of LSTM on WikiCoref, by adding the words from the WikiCoref dataset into its dictionary. The LSTM model trained with this extended dictionary is denoted as *LSTM*† in Table 2. *LSTM*† results are still lower than those of the SVM model while SVM does not use any information from the test dataset. Pruning rare lexical features from the training data along the incorporation of part of speech tags, which are far more generalizable than lexical features, could explain the generalizability of the SVM model on the new domain.

	Non-Anaphoric			Anaphoric		
	R	P	F1	R	P	F1
LSTM	95.53	89.88	92.62	69.50	84.58	76.31
LSTM†	93.25	92.78	93.01	79.41	80.57	79.99
SVM	93.83	93.05	93.43	80.11	82.07	81.08

Table 2: Results on the WikiCoref dataset.

5 Analysis Based on Mention Types

We analyze the output of the LSTM and SVM models on the CoNLL 2012 test set to see how well they perform for different types of mentions. As can be seen from Table 3, there is not much difference between the performance of LSTM and SVM for recognizing anaphoric pronouns. SVM detects anaphoric proper names better while LSTM is better at recognizing anaphoric common nouns.

We also analyze the output of LSTM*. As can be seen, the incorporation of surface features does not affect the detection of anaphoric pronouns very much while it mainly affects the detection of anaphoric proper names by about 24 percent.

In order to see whether the same pattern holds for coreference resolution, we compare the recall and precision errors of the best coreference system that only uses surface features, i.e. cort (Martschat and Strube, 2015) with singleton features (Moosavi and Strube, 2016) [2], and the state-of-the-art deep coreference resolver, i.e. deep-coref (Clark and Manning, 2016a). The comparison of the errors for the CoNLL 2012 test set is shown in Table 4. We use the error analysis tool of cort introduced by Martschat and Strube (2014) for the results of Table 4. As can be seen from Table 4, while deep-coref is significantly better than cort for resolving common nouns and specially pronouns, its result does not go far beyond that of cort when it comes to resolving proper names.

	Anaphoric					
	R	P	F1	R	P	F1
	Proper names			Common nouns		
LSTM	79.49	82.31	80.88	62.96	65.04	63.99
LSTM*	47.60	70.09	56.69	46.30	57.75	51.40
SVM	83.80	85.71	84.74	52.46	71.98	60.69
	Pronouns			Other		
LSTM	94.67	85.60	89.91	29.11	63.88	40.00
LSTM*	92.67	86.01	89.22	10.13	34.78	15.69
SVM	95.59	86.29	90.71	32.91	76.47	46.02

Table 3: Anaphoricity results for each mention type on the CoNLL 2012 test set.

6 Discussion

In this paper we analyze the effect of surface features for anaphoricity detection, which is a small but an important step for coreference resolution.

[2]Available at https://github.com/ns-moosavi/cort/tree/singleton_feature

	Name	Noun	Pronoun
	#Recall Errors		
deep-coref	1110	1499	1537
cort	1145	1638	1655
	#Precision Errors		
deep-coref	713	672	1162
cort	738	747	1736

Table 4: Coreference error analysis.

Our analysis shows that surface features, as it was known, are important. Based on our results, the effects of incorporating surface properties and generalized representations are different for different types of mentions. These results suggest that apart from a unified model, we should consider different models or at least different features for processing different types of mentions and do not put all the burden on a single model to learn the differences. The works by Lassalle and Denis (2013) and Denis and Baldridge (2008) are examples of models in which distinct models have been used for various types of mentions. Besides, our analysis shows the importance of surface features for proper names. Word embeddings are very useful for capturing semantic relatedness. A coreference resolver that uses word embeddings has a great advantage in better resolution of common nouns and pronouns. However, the use of surface features in current state-of-the-art coreference resolvers is very limited. Before going towards using more sophisticated knowledge sources, there are still easy victories that can be achieved by incorporating more generalizable surface properties, especially for proper names.

Acknowledgments

The authors would like to thank Kevin Clark for his help with the deep-coref software and Mark-Christoph Müller for his helpful comments. We would also like to thank the four anonymous reviewers for their detailed comments on an earlier draft of the paper. This work has been funded by the Klaus Tschira Foundation, Heidelberg, Germany. The first author has been supported by a Heidelberg Institute for Theoretical Studies PhD. scholarship.

References

Shane Bergsma and David Yarowsky. 2011. NADA: A robust system for non-referential pronoun detection. In *Anaphora Processing and Applications. Proceedings of the 8th Discourse Anaphora and Anaphor Resolution Colloquium*, Lisbon, Portugal, 6-7 October 2011, pages 12–23. Springer, Heidelberg.

Shane Bergsma, Dekang Lin, and Randy Goebel. 2008. Distributional identification of non-referential pronouns. In *Proceedings of the 46th Annual Meeting of the Association for Computational Linguistics: Human Language Technologies*, Columbus, Ohio, 15–20 June 2008, pages 10–18.

Donna Byron and Whitney Gegg-Harrison. 2004. Eliminating non-referring noun phrases from coreference resolution. In *Proceedings the Discourse Anaphora and Reference Resolution Conference*, pages 21–26.

Kevin Clark and Christopher D. Manning. 2016a. Improving coreference resolution by learning entity-level distributed representations. In *Proceedings of the 54th Annual Meeting of the Association for Computational Linguistics (Volume 1: Long Papers)*, pages 643–653, Berlin, Germany, August. Association for Computational Linguistics.

Kevin Clark and Christopher D. Manning. 2016b. Deep reinforcement learning for mention-ranking coreference models. In *Proceedings of the 2016 Conference on Empirical Methods in Natural Language Processing*, pages 2256–2262, Austin, Texas, November. Association for Computational Linguistics.

Pascal Denis and Jason Baldridge. 2008. Specialized models and ranking for coreference resolution. In *Proceedings of the 2008 Conference on Empirical Methods in Natural Language Processing*, Waikiki, Honolulu, Hawaii, 25–27 October 2008, pages 660–669.

Richard Evans. 2001. Applying machine learning toward an automatic classification of it. *Literary and Linguistic Computing*, 16(1):45–57.

Abbas Ghaddar and Philippe Langlais. 2016. WikiCoref: An English coreference-annotated corpus of Wikipedia articles. In *Proceedings of the Tenth International Conference on Language Resources and Evaluation (LREC 2016)*, Portorož, Slovenia, 05/2016.

Yoav Goldberg and Michael Elhadad. 2007. SVM model tampering and anchored learning: a case study in Hebrew NP chunking. *Proceedings of the 45th Annual Meeting of the Association for Computational Linguistics*, pages 224–231.

Yoav Goldberg and Michael Elhadad. 2009. On the role of lexical features in sequence labeling. In *Proceedings of the 2009 Conference on Empirical Methods in Natural Language Processing*, Singapore, 6–7 August 2009, pages 1142–1151. Association for Computational Linguistics.

Geoffrey E. Hinton, Nitish Srivastava, Alex Krizhevsky, Ilya Sutskever, and Ruslan R. Salakhutdinov. 2012. Improving neural networks by preventing co-adaptation of feature detectors. *arXiv preprint arXiv:1207.0580*.

Sepp Hochreiter and Jürgen Schmidhuber. 1997. Long short-term memory. *Neural Computation*, 9(8):1735–1780.

Diederik Kingma and Jimmy Ba. 2014. Adam: A method for stochastic optimization. *arXiv preprint arXiv:1412.6980*.

Emmanuel Lassalle and Pascal Denis. 2013. Improving pairwise coreference models through feature space hierarchy learning. In *Proceedings of the 51st Annual Meeting of the Association for Computational Linguistics (Volume 1: Long Papers)*, Sofia, Bulgaria, 4–9 August 2013, pages 497–506.

Emmanuel Lassalle and Pascal Denis. 2015. Joint anaphoricity detection and coreference resolution with constrained latent structures. In *Proceedings of the 29th Conference on the Advancement of Artificial Intelligence*, Austin, Texas, 25–30 January 2015, pages 2274–2280.

Marie-Catherine de Marneffe, Marta Recasens, and Christopher Potts. 2015. Modeling the lifespan of discourse entities with application to coreference resolution. *Journal of Artificial Intelligent Research*, 52:445–475.

Sebastian Martschat and Michael Strube. 2014. Recall error analysis for coreference resolution. In *Proceedings of the 2014 Conference on Empirical Methods in Natural Language Processing*, Doha, Qatar, 25–29 October 2014, pages 2070–2081.

Sebastian Martschat and Michael Strube. 2015. Latent structures for coreference resolution. *Transactions of the Association for Computational Linguistics*, 3:405–418.

Nafise Sadat Moosavi and Michael Strube. 2016. Search space pruning: A simple solution for better coreference resolvers. In *Proceedings of the 2016 Conference of the North American Chapter of the Association for Computational Linguistics: Human Language Technologies*, San Diego, Cal., 12–17 June 2016, pages 1005–1011.

Christoph Müller. 2006. Automatic detection of nonreferential *it* in spoken multi-party dialog. In *Proceedings of the 11th Conference of the European Chapter of the Association for Computational Linguistics*, Trento, Italy, 3–7 April 2006. 49-56.

Vincent Ng and Claire Cardie. 2002. Identifying anaphoric and non-anaphoric noun phrases to improve coreference resolution. In *Proceedings of the 19th International Conference on Computational Linguistics*, Taipei, Taiwan, 24 August – 1 September 2002, pages 730–736.

Vincent Ng. 2004. Learning noun phrase anaphoricity to improve coreference resolution. In *Proceedings of the 42nd Annual Meeting of the Association for Computational Linguistics*, Barcelona, Spain, 21–26 July 2004, pages 151–158.

Vincent Ng. 2009. Graph-cut-based anaphoricity determination for coreference resolution. In *Proceedings of Human Language Technologies 2009: The Conference of the North American Chapter of the Association for Computational Linguistics*, Boulder, Col., 31 May – 5 June 2009, pages 575–583.

Jeffrey Pennington, Richard Socher, and Christopher D. Manning. 2014. GloVe: Global vectors for word representation. In *Proceedings of the 2014 Conference on Empirical Methods in Natural Language Processing*, Doha, Qatar, 25–29 October 2014, pages 1532–1543.

Ellen F. Prince. 1992. The ZPG letter: Subjects, definiteness, and information-status. In W.C. Mann and S.A. Thompson, editors, *Discourse Description. Diverse Linguistic Analyses of a Fund-Raising Text*, pages 295–325. John Benjamins, Amsterdam.

Marta Recasens, Marie-Catherine de Marneffe, and Christopher Potts. 2013. The life and death of discourse entities: Identifying singleton mentions. In *Proceedings of the 2013 Conference of the North American Chapter of the Association for Computational Linguistics: Human Language Technologies*, Atlanta, Georgia, 9–14 June 2013, pages 627–633.

Ilya Sutskever, Oriol Vinyals, and Quoc V. Le. 2014. Sequence to sequence learning with neural networks. *Advances in Neural Information Processing Systems*, pages 3104–3112.

Olga Uryupina. 2009. Detecting Anaphoricity and Antecedenthood for Coreference Resolution. *Procesamiento del Lenguaje Natural*, 42.

Kees van Deemter and Rodger Kibble. 2000. On coreferring: Coreference in MUC and related annotation schemes. *Computational Linguistics*, 26(4):629–637.

Oriol Vinyals, Lukasz Kaiser, Terry Koo, Slav Petrov, Ilya Sutskever, and Geoffrey Hinton. 2014. Grammar as a foreign language. *arXiv preprint arXiv:1412.7449*.

Sam Wiseman, Alexander M. Rush, Stuart Shieber, and Jason Weston. 2015. Learning anaphoricity and antecedent ranking features for coreference resolution. In *Proceedings of the 53rd Annual Meeting of the Association for Computational Linguistics (Volume 1: Long Papers)*, Beijing, China, 26–31 July 2015, pages 1416–1426.

Sam Wiseman, Alexander M. Rush, and Stuart Shieber. 2016. Learning global features for coreference resolution. In *Proceedings of the 2016 Conference of the North American Chapter of the Association for*

Computational Linguistics: Human Language Technologies, San Diego, Cal., 12–17 June 2016. To appear.

Guodong Zhou and Fang Kong. 2009. Global learning of noun phrase anaphoricity in coreference resolution via label propagation. In *Proceedings of the 2009 Conference on Empirical Methods in Natural Language Processing,* Singapore, 6–7 August 2009, pages 978–986.

Enriching Basque Coreference Resolution System using Semantic Knowledge sources

Ander Soraluze and **Olatz Arregi** and **Xabier Arregi** and **Arantza Díaz de Ilarraza**
University of the Basque Country
Donostia - San Sebastián, Spain
{ander.soraluze,olatz.arregi, xabier.arregi,a.diazdeilarraza}@ehu.eus

Abstract

In this paper we present a Basque coreference resolution system enriched with semantic knowledge. An error analysis carried out revealed the deficiencies that the system had in resolving coreference cases in which semantic or world knowledge is needed. We attempt to improve the deficiencies using two semantic knowledge sources, specifically Wikipedia and WordNet.

1 Introduction

Coreference resolution consists of identifying textual expressions (mentions) that refer to real-world objects (entities) and determining which of these mentions refer to the same entity. While different string-matching techniques are useful to determine which of these mentions refer to the same entity, there are cases in which more knowledge is needed, that is the case of the Example in 1.

(1) [**Osasunak**] lehenengo mailara igotzeko lehian azken astean bizi duen giroa oso polita da. [**Taldea**] lasaitzeko asmoz Oronozera eraman zituen Lotinak atzo guztiak. Oronozko kontzentrazioa beharrezkoa dute [**gorritxoek**].

*"[**Osasuna**] is going through a beautiful moment in the last week in the race to ascend to the Premier League. In order to reassure [**the team**] Lotina has decided to give all of them to Oronoz. [**The reds**] need to concentrate in Oronoz."*

Having the world knowledge that *Osasuna* is a *football team* and its nickname is *the reds* would be helpful for establishing the coreference relations between the mentions [**Osasuna**], [**Taldea**] and [**gorritxoek**] in the example presented above.

Evaluation scores used in coreference resolution tasks can show how effective a system is; however, they neither identify deficiencies of the system, nor give any indication of how those errors might be corrected. Error analyses are a good option that can help to clear the deficiencies of a coreference resolver. Bearing this in mind, we have carried out an error analysis of the extended version of the coreference resolution system presented in Soraluze et al. (2015). In this paper we present an improvement of this Basque coreference resolution system by using semantic knowledge sources in order to correctly resolve cases like in Example 1.

This paper is structured as follows. After presenting an error analysis of the coreference resolution system in Section 2, we analyse similar works to ours in which semantic knowledge sources have been used to improve coreference resolution in Section 3. Section 4 presents how we integrated the semantic knowledge in our system. The main experimental results are outlined in Section 5 and discussed in Section 6. Finally, we review the main conclusions and preview future work.

2 Error Analysis

A deep error-analysis can reveal the weak points of the coreference resolution system and help to decide future directions in the improvement of the system. The system we have evaluated is an adaptation of the Stanford Coreference resolution system (Lee et al., 2013) to the Basque language. The Stanford coreference resolution module is a deterministic rule-based system which is based on ten independent coreference models or sieves that are precision-oriented, i.e., they are applied sequentially from highest to lowest precision. All the sieves of the system have been modified taking into account the characteristics of the Basque lan-

Proceedings of the 2nd Workshop on Coreference Resolution Beyond OntoNotes (CORBON 2017), co-located with EACL 2017, pages 8–16,
Valencia, Spain, April 4, 2017. ©2017 Association for Computational Linguistics

guage and, one new sieve has been added, obtaining an end-to-end coreference resolution system.

The corpus used to carry out the error analysis is a part of EPEC (the Reference Corpus for the Processing of Basque) (Aduriz et al., 2006). EPEC is a 300,000 word sample collection of news published in *Euskaldunon Egunkaria*, a Basque language newspaper. The part of the corpus we have used has about 45,000 words and it has been manually tagged at coreference level by two linguists (Ceberio et al., 2016). First of all, automatically tagged mentions obtained by a mention detector (Soraluze et al., 2016) have been corrected; then, coreferent mentions have been linked in clusters.

More detailed information about the EPEC corpus can be found in Table 1.

	Words	Mentions	Clusters	Singletons
Devel	30434	8432	1313	4383
Test	15949	4360	621	2445

Table 1: EPEC corpus division information

2.1 Error types

The errors have been classified following the categorization presented in Kummerfeld and Klein (2013). The tool[1] presented in the paper has been used to help in identifying and quantifying the errors produced by the coreference resolution system:

- **Span Error (SE):** A mention span has been identified incorrectly.
- **Conflated Entities (CE):** Two entities have been unified creating a new incorrect one.
- **Extra Mention (EM):** An entity includes an incorrectly identified mention.
- **Extra Entity (EE):** An entity which consists of incorrectly identified mentions is outputted by the system.
- **Divided Entity (DE):** An entity has been divided in two entities.
- **Missing Mention (MM):** A not identified mention is missing in an entity.
- **Missing Entity (ME):** The system misses an entity which is present in the gold standard.

The error types are summarised in Table 2.

[1]code.google.com/p/berkeley-coreference-analyser/

Error Type	System	Gold
Span Error	s_1	s_1 s_2
Conflated Entities	$\{m_1, m_2\}_{e1}$ -	$\{m_1\}_{e1}$ $\{m_2\}_{e2}$
Extra Mention	$\{m_1, m_2\}$	$\{m_1\}$
Extra Entity	$\{m_1, m_2\}$	-
Divided Entity	$\{m_1\}_{e1}$ $\{m_2\}_{e2}$	$\{m_1, m_2\}_{e1}$ -
Missing Mention	$\{m_1\}$	$\{m_1, m_2\}$
Missing Entity	-	$\{m_1, m_2\}$

Table 2: Error types. s=string, m=mention, e=entity

2.2 Error causes

Apart from classifying the errors committed by the coreference resolution system, it is important to observe the causes of these error types. These are the causes of errors we found:

- **Preprocessing (PP):** Errors in the preprocessing step (lemmatization, PoS tagging, etc.) provoke incorrect or missing links in coreference resolution.
- **Mention Detection (MD):** These errors are provoked due to incorrectly identified (not a mention, incorrect boundaries..) or missed mentions during mention detection step. Missed mentions directly affect the recall of the system, and incorrectly identified mentions affect precision.
- **Pronominal Resolution (PR):** The system often generates incorrect links between the pronoun and its antecedent.
- **Ellipsis Resolution (ER):** Elliptical mentions do not provide much information as they omit the noun, as a consequence it is difficult to correctly link these types of mentions with their correct antecedent.

  For example, it is complicated to link the elliptical mention [Yosi Beilin Israelgo Justizia ministroak Jeruralemi buruz esandako-Ø[2]-ak] "what Yosi Beilin Israel Justice Minister said" with its antecedent [Beilin Justizia ministroaren hitzak] "Beilin Justice minister's words".
- **Semantic Knowledge (SK):** Errors related to a semantic relation (synonymy, hyperonymy, metonymy) between the heads of two mentions.

[2]In this case Ø refers to "what".

For example, in mentions [Libanoko Parlamentuak] "Lebanon parliament" and [Libanoko Legebiltzarrak] "Lebanon parliament", *parlamentua* is a synomyn of *legebiltzarra*.

- **World Knowledge (WK):** In some cases the system is not able to link mentions as a consequence of the lack of world knowledge required to resolve them correctly.

  For example, to link the mention [Reala] "Reala" with the mention [talde txuri-urdinak] "white-blue team", it is necessary to know that *Reala* is a team and the nickname of the football team is *txuri-urdinak* "white-blue".

- **Miscellaneous (MISC):** In this category we classify the errors that are not contained in the above categories.

  An example of a miscellaneous error could be the following. The mention [Kelme, Euskaltel eta Lampre] should be linked with the mention [Hiru taldeak] "The three teams". In this specific example it is necessary to know that Kelme, Euskaltel and Lampre are teams and the enumerated mention has three elements.

After defining the error types and the error causes, we analysed how the error causes affect the error types in EPEC corpus. The distribution of errors is shown in Figure 1.

As we observe in Figure 1, the most common errors types of the system fail in Span Error (29.36%), Conflated Entities (11.92%), Divided Entities (42.88%) and Missing Mention (11.92%) categories.

Observing the error causes, we can conclude that mention detection is crucial for coreference resolution, 52.52% of errors. Improving mention detection would likely improve the scores obtained in coreference resolution. Nevertheless, in order to identify deficiencies of a coreference resolution system, Pronominal Resolution (9.17%), Ellipsis Resolution (3.21%), Semantics (6.42%) and World Knowledge (9.86%) categories can reveal how the errors might be corrected. Due to the variety of errors classified in miscellaneous category, little improvement would be achieved despite making a big effort to solve them.

Among all the error causes, in this paper we are going to focus on errors provoked by the lack of semantic and world knowledge.

3 Related Work

Lexical and encyclopedic information sources, such as WordNet, Wikipedia, Yago or DBPedia have been widely used to improve coreference resolution.

WordNet (Fellbaum, 1998) is the one of oldest resources for lexical knowledge. It consists of *synsets*, which link synonymous word senses together. Using WordNet's structure, it is possible to find synonyms and hyperonymic relations. Wikipedia is a collaborative open source encyclopedia edited by volunteers and provides a very large domain-independent encyclopedic repository. Yago (Suchanek et al., 2007) is a knowledge base, linking Wikipedia entries to the WordNet ontology. And finally, DBPedia (Mendes et al., 2012) contains useful ontological information extracted from the data in Wikipedia.

Regarding works in which lexical and encyclopedic information sources have been exploited, Ponzetto and Strube (2006) were the earliest to use WordNet and Wikipedia.

Uryupina et al. (2011) extracted semantic compatibility and aliasing information from Wikipedia and Yago and incorporated it in coreference resolution system. They showed that using such knowledge with no disambiguation and filtering does not bring any improvement over the baseline, whereas a few very simple disambiguation and filtering techniques lead to better results. In the end, they improve their system's performance by 2-3 percentage points.

Rahman and Ng (2011) used Yago to inject knowledge attributes in mentions, but noticed that knowledge injection could be noisy.

Durrett and Klein (2013) observed that the semantic information contained even in a coreference corpus of thousands of documents is insufficient to generalize to unseen data, so system designers have turned to external resources. Using specialised features, as well as WordNet-based hypernymy and synonymy and other resources, they obtained a gain from 60.06 in CoNLL score to 61.58 using automatic mentions, and from 75.08 to 76.68 with gold mentions.

Ratinov and Roth (2012) extract attributes from Wikipedia pages which they used to improve the recall in their system, based on a hybrid (Lee et al., 2013).

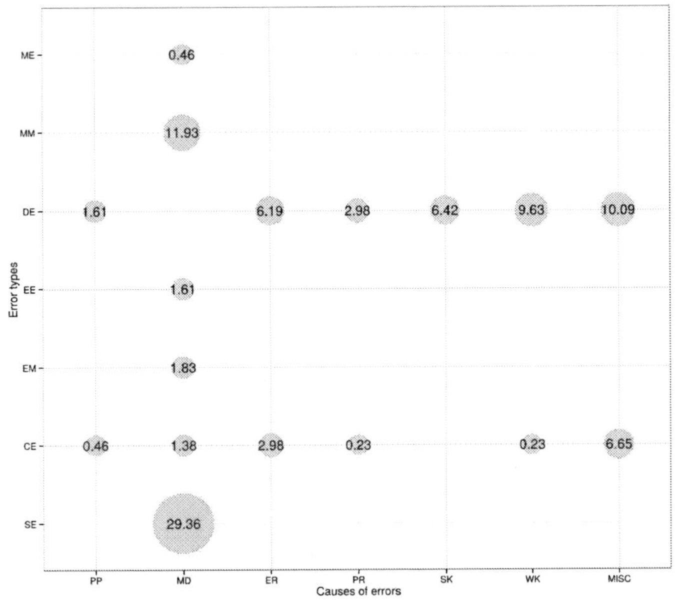

Figure 1: Distribution of error causes into error types.

In Hajishirzi et al. (2013) NECo, a new model for named entity linking and coreference resolution, which solves both problems jointly, reducing the errors of each is introduced. NECo extends the Stanford deterministic coreference resolution system by automatically linking mentions to Wikipedia and introducing new sieves which profit from information obtained by named entity linking.

As pointed out in Recasens et al. (2013), opaque mentions (mentions with very different words like *Google* and *the search giant*) account for 65% of the errors made by state-of-the-art systems, so to improve coreference scores beyond 60-70% it is necessary to make better use of semantic and world knowledge to deal with non-identical-string coreference. They use a corpus of comparable documents to extract aliases and they report that their method not only finds synonymy and instance relations, but also metonymic cases. They obtain a gain of 0.7% F1 score for the CoNLL metric using gold mentions.

Lee et al. (2013) mention that the biggest challenge in coreference resolution, accounting for 42% of errors in the state-of-the art Stanford system, is the inability to reason effectively about background semantic knowledge.

The intuition behind the work presented in Durrett and Klein (2014) is that named entity recognition on ambiguous instances can obtain benefit using coreference resolution, and similarly can benefit from Wikipedia knowledge. At the same time, coreference can profit from better named entity information.

4 Improving Coreference Resolution with Semantic Knowledge sources

This section explains the improvement process of the coreference resolution system with semantic knowledge sources. In order to treat cases where knowledge is needed, two new specialised sieves have been added to the coreference resolution system: One to extract knowledge from Wikipedia and the other to obtain semantic information from WordNet.

4.1 Enriching mentions with Named Entity Linking

Named Entity Linking is the task of matching mentions to corresponding entities in a knowledge base, such as Wikipedia.

As pointed out in Versley et al. (2016), named entity linking, or disambiguation of entity mentions, is beneficial to make full use of the information in Wikipedia.

The Basque version of Wikipedia, contained

about 258,000 articles in September 2016, which is much smaller in size when compared with English Wikipedia, which contained about 5,250,837 pages on the same date.

In order to disambiguate and link mentions to Basque Wikipedia pages, the following formula has been applied to all the named entity mentions in a document:

$$P(s, c, e) = P(e \mid s)P(e \mid c)$$

$P(e \mid s)$ is the probability of being entity e given s string, i.e., the normalised probability of being entity e linked with string s in Wikipedia. $P(e \mid c)$ is the probability of being entity e given the context c. The context c is a window of size $[-50, +50]$ of the string s. To calculate $P(e \mid c)$ probability, UKB[3] software has been utilised. UKB software uses *Personalized Page Rank* algorithm presented in (Agirre and Soroa, 2009) and (Agirre et al., 2014) to estimate the probabilities.

If a named-entity mention is linked with any page from Wikipedia, the page that UKB says it is the most probable is used to enrich the mention. From the Wikipedia page the following information is obtained:

- The title of the page. The title sometimes gives useful information. For example, for the named-entity mention *AEK*, the title of its Wikipedia page is *Alfabetatze Euskalduntze Koordinakundea* "Literacy and Euskaldunization Coordinator", where the extent of the acronym is obtained. Furthermore it gives the information that AEK is a coordinator, *koordinakundea*.

- The first sentence. The first paragraph of each Wikipedia article provides a very brief summary of the entity. Usually the most useful information is in the first sentence, this is where the entity is defined.

- If the Wikipedia page has an Infobox, we extract information from it. Infoboxes contain structured information in which the attributes of many entities are listed in a standardized way.

After the information is obtained from the Wikipedia page, this information is processed and the NPs are extracted.

[3]http://ixa2.si.ehu.es/ukb/

These NPs and their sub-phrases are used to enrich the mentions with world knowledge. To further reduce the noise, the NPs that are location named-entities in a Wikipedia page about a location are discarded.

Taking Example 1, the mention *Osasuna* is enriched as follows: The most probable Wikipedia page proposed by UKB for the mention *Osasuna* is *Osasuna_futbol_kluba* "Osasuna football club". Therefore, we obtain from this page the title, the first sentence and Infobox information. The NPs obtained after the information is processed are *gorritxoak* "the reds", *Osasuna futbol kluba* "Osasuna football club" and *Nafarroako futbol taldea* "football team from Navarre". So the mention *Osasuna* is enriched with the set of lemmas of the NPs and the lemmas of their sub-phrases: {gorritxo, Osasuna futbol klub, futbol klub, klub, Nafarroa futbol talde, futbol talde, talde} "{the reds, Osasuna football club, football club, club, football team from Navarre, football team, team}".

4.2 Wiki-alias sieve

The new Wiki-alias sieve uses the mentions enriched by information obtained from Wikipedia pages.

Using this information, the Wiki-alias sieve assumes that two mentions are coreferent if one of the two following conditions is fulfilled:

i) the set of enriched word lemmas in the potential antecedent has all the mention candidate's span lemmas. To better understand this constraint, suppose that the mention *Realak* is enriched with {talde, futbol talde, txuri-urdin} "{team, football team, white and blue}", as the potential antecedent *Realak* has all the lemmas in the mention candidate's span, i.e., *talde* "{team}" and *txuri-urdin* "{white and blue}", the mention *talde txuri-urdinak* "{white and blue team}" is considered coreferent of *Realak*.

ii) the head word lemma of the mention candidate is equal to the head word lemma of the potential antecedent or equal to any lemma in the set of enriched lemmas of the potential antecedent, and all the enriched lemmas of the potential antecedent appear in the cluster lemmas of the mention candidate. For example, this constraint considers coreferent the potential antecedent *Jacques Chiracek* and the mention candidate *Jacques Chirac Frantziako errepublikako presidentea*. After *Jacques Chiracek* mention has been enriched with lemmas {presidente, Frantzia presidente} "{president, France president}", the head word lemma of the mention candidate *presidente* is equal to a lemma in the set of enriched lemmas of the potential antecedent *presidente* and all the enriched lemmas of the potential antecedent appear in the cluster lemmas of the mention candidate, so the second constraint is fulfilled. This constraint aims to link coreferent mentions where a mention with novel information appears later in text than the less informative one. As pointed out in Fox (1993), it is not common to introduce novel information in later mentions but it sometimes happens.

4.3 Synonymy sieve

To create this new sieve, we have extracted from Basque WordNet (Pociello et al., 2011) all the words that are considered synonyms in this ontology. The Basque WordNet contains 32,456 synsets and 26,565 lemmas, and is complemented by a hand-tagged corpus comprising 59,968 annotations (Pociello et al., 2011).

From all synsets, a static list of 16,771 sets of synonyms has been created and integrated in the coreference resolution system. Using the synonyms' static list, the *Synonymy sieve* considers two mentions as coreferent if the following constraints are fulfilled: i) the head word of the potential antecedent and the head word of the mention candidate are synonyms and ii) all the lemmas in the mention candidate's span are in the potential antecedent cluster word lemmas or *vice versa*. For example, the mention candidate *Libanoko legebiltzarra* "Lebanon parliament" and the *Libanoko parlametua* "Lebanon parliament" are considered coreferent as the head words *legebiltzarra* and *parlamentua* are synonyms and the lemma *Libano* "Lebanon" of the word *Libanoko* is present in the cluster word lemmas of the potential antecedent.

5 System evaluation

In order to quantify the impact of using semantic knowledge sources in coreference resolution, we have tested the enriched coreference resolution system using the EPEC corpus and compared the results with the baseline system. The experimentation has been carried out using automatic mentions and gold mentions. In both cases named entity disambiguation and entity linking has been performed automatically.

5.1 Metrics

The metrics used to evaluate the systems' performances are MUC (Vilain et al., 1995), B^3 (Bagga and Baldwin, 1998), CEAF$_e$ (Luo, 2005), CEAF$_m$ (Luo, 2005), BLANC (Recasens and Hovy, 2011) and LEA (Moosavi and Strube, 2016). The CoNLL metrics is the arithmetic mean of MUC, B^3 and CEAF$_e$ metrics. The scores have been calculated using the reference implementation of the CoNLL scorer (Pradhan et al., 2014).

5.2 Experimental results

As pointed out in Rahman and Ng (2011), while different knowledge sources have been shown to be useful when applied in isolation to a coreference system, it is also interesting to observe if they offer complementary benefits and can therefore further improve a resolver when applied in combination. In order to quantify the individual improvement of each new sieve, we compared the baseline system (1) with the system in which the wiki-alias sieve has been added (2), with the one where the synonymy sieve has been added (3), and with the final system combining both sieves (4).

Table 3 shows the results obtained by the baseline system compared with those obtained by the coreference resolution system, which uses semantic knowledge sources. These scores are obtained with automatically detected mentions (F_1 =77.57).

The scores obtained by systems using the gold mentions (F_1 =100), i.e., when providing all the correct mentions to the coreference resolution systems, are shown in Table 4.

6 Discussion

Observing the results presented in Table 3, we can see that the baseline system's F_1 scores are outperformed in all the metrics by the semantically enriched system. In CoNLL metric, the improved system has a score of 55.81, which is slightly higher than the baseline system, to be precise, 0.24 higher.

As shown in Table 4, the baseline F_1 scores are also outperformed in all the metrics, except in B^3 when gold mentions are used. The official CoNLL metric is improved by 0.39 points.

Regarding recall and precision scores when automatic and gold mentions are used, all the metrics

	Automatic Mentions																		
	MUC			B^3			$CEAF_m$			$CEAF_e$			BLANC			LEA			CoNLL
	R	P	F1	R	P	F1	R	P	F1	R	P	F1	R	P	F1	R	P	F1	F1
1	34.1	55.76	42.32	57.98	68.83	62.94	60.78	62.31	61.54	66.02	58.41	61.98	38.41	53.57	43.18	46.71	51.78	49.12	55.74
2	34.41	55.70	42.54	58.09	68.64	62.93	60.73	62.26	61.49	65.94	58.49	61.99	38.65	53.27	43.35	46.82	51.64	49.11	55.82
3	34.57	56.03	42.76	58.08	68.80	62.98	60.85	62.38	61.61	65.99	58.51	62.03	38.53	53.65	43.31	46.83	51.97	49.27	55.92
4	34.88	55.90	**42.95***	58.19	68.60	**62.97**	60.80	62.33	**61.56**	65.92	58.60	**62.04**	38.77	53.33	**43.48***	46.94	51.83	**49.26**	**55.98***

Table 3: Results obtained when automatic mentions are used. 1=Baseline, 2=1+Wiki sieve, 3=2+Synonymy sieve, 4=1+Wiki sieve+Synonymy sieve.

	Gold Mentions																		
	MUC			B^3			$CEAF_m$			$CEAF_e$			BLANC			LEA			CoNLL
	R	P	F1	R	P	F1	R	P	F1	R	P	F1	R	P	F1	R	P	F1	F1
1	48.76	71.94	58.12	81.35	93.47	86.99	80.57	80.57	80.57	89.00	78.24	83.27	67.09	84.65	72.77	66.36	71.11	68.66	76.12
2	49.84	70.81	58.50	81.71	92.83	86.92	80.57	80.57	80.57	88.69	78.77	83.44	67.51	83.27	72.84	66.60	71.01	68.73	76.28
3	50.00	71.50	58.85	81.69	93.19	87.06	80.80	80.80	80.80	88.90	78.82	83.56	67.39	84.23	72.95	66.68	71.52	69.02	76.49
4	50.46	70.99	**58.99***	81.86	92.81	86.99	80.71	80.71	**80.71**	88.71	79.00	**83.57***	67.68	83.34	**73.00**	66.79	71.29	**68.97**	**76.51***

Table 4: Results obtained when gold mentions are used. 1=Baseline, 2=1+Wiki sieve, 3=2+Synonymy sieve, 4=1+Wiki sieve+Synonymy sieve.

except CEAF$_e$ show an improvement in recall and decrease in precision when two new sieves are applied. The reason why the CEAF$_e$ metric is behaving differently could be that, as mentioned by Denis and Baldridge (2009), CEAF ignores all correct decisions of unaligned response entities. Consequently, the CEAF metric may lead to unreliable results.

It is interesting to compare the improvements obtained by the system which uses semantic knowledge sources in CoNLL scores. The improvement when automatic mentions are used is lower than when gold mentions are provided, 0.24 and 0.39 respectively. In both cases, even the improvements obtained are modest, they are statistically significant using Paired Student's t-test with p-value < 0.05.

As pointed out in Versley et al. (2016), in realistic settings, where the loss in precision would be amplified by the additional non-gold mentions, it is substantially harder to achieve gains by incorporate lexical and encyclopedic knowledge, but possible and necessary. A similar idea is concluded by Durrett and Klein (2013). They mention that despite the fact that absolute performance numbers are much higher on gold mentions and there is less room for improvement, the semantic features help much more than they do in system mentions.

To conclude the analysis of the results, it is also interesting to observe the difference between the results obtained by both systems when automatic mentions and when gold mentions are used. It is clear that having accurate preprocessing tools and a good mention detector are crucial to obtain good results in coreference resolution. In both systems the difference in CoNLL score is about 20.00 points higher when gold mentions are used.

The results obtained have enabled us to carry out a new error analysis in the development set. After applying the new two sieves, the error analysis has revealed four major issues that directly affect not obtaining bigger improvement when knowledge resources are used:

1. Some mentions do not have Wikipedia entry, as the coverage of Basque Wikipedia (257,546 pages) has less coverage than other languages, for example English (5,250,837 pages), i.e., Basque version is 21 times smaller.

2. Due to incorrect mention disambiguation, some mentions are linked to incorrect Wikipedia pages. The precision obtained in disambiguation is 87,84%.

3. Precision errors, provoked by cases where many proper noun mentions were potential antecedent for a common noun. For example, *Oslo* is linked by *hiriburu* "capital", nevertheless the correct antecedent for *hiriburu* is another capital that appears in text, in this specific case, *Jerusalem*.

4. Some indefinite mentions which do not have antecedent are linked incorrectly. For example, *estaturik* "state" is linked with *Frantziak* "France".

5. In the synonyms' static list, some synonyms that appear in texts are missing. In addition, many synonyms are so generic, i.e., they

are synonyms depending on the context in which they appear. As a consequence of missing synonyms, some mentions with synonymy relations between them are not linked. The presence of very generic synonyms provokes to incorrectly link mentions that are not coreferent, so that precision decreases. Identifying the particular sense that a word has in context would likely help to improve the precision.

Regarding the issues that affect improvement of the systems when knowledge bases are used, Uryupina et al. (2011) suggest that in their particular case the errors introduced are not caused by any deficiencies in web knowledge bases, but reflect the complex nature of the coreference resolution task.

7 Conclusions and future work

We have enriched the Basque coreference resolution adding new two sieves, *Wiki-alias* and *Synonymy sieve*, respectively. The first sieve uses the enriched information of named-entity mentions after they have been linked to their correspondent Wikipedia page, using Entity Linking techniques. The second sieve uses a static list of synonyms extracted from Basque WordNet to consider whether two mentions are coreferent.

Applying the two new sieves, the system obtains an improvement of 0.24 points in CoNLL F_1 when automatic mentions are used and the CoNLL score is outperformed by 0.39 points when the gold mentions are provided. The error analysis of the enriched system has revealed that the knowledge bases used, Basque Wikipedia and Basque WordNet, have deficiencies in their coverage compared with knowledge bases in major languages, for example, English. We suggest that there is margin of improvement, as Basque Wikipedia and Basque WordNet coverage increase, bearing in mind that coreference resolution is a complex task.

As future work, we intend to improve the Pronoun resolution and Ellipsis Resolution, as we observed in the error analysis presented in Section 2 they are the cause of considerable coreference resolution errors, around % 12 of total errors.

Acknowledgments

This work has been supported by first author's PhD grant from Euskara Errektoreordetza, the University of the Basque Country (UPV/EHU) and by the EXTRECM project, Spanish Government (TIN2013-46616-C2-1-R).

References

Itziar Aduriz, María Jesús Aranzabe, Jose Mari Arriola, Maite Atutxa, Arantza Díaz de Ilarraza, Nerea Ezeiza, Koldo Gojenola, Maite Oronoz, Aitor Soroa, and Ruben Urizar. 2006. Methodology and Steps towards the Construction of EPEC, a Corpus of Written Basque Tagged at Morphological and Syntactic Levels for the Automatic Processing. In *Language and Computers*, volume 56, pages 1–15. Rodopi, Amsterdam, Netherlands.

Eneko Agirre and Aitor Soroa. 2009. Personalizing PageRank for Word Sense Disambiguation. In *Proceedings of the 12th Conference of the European Chapter of the Association for Computational Linguistics*, EACL '09, pages 33–41, Athens, Greece. Association for Computational Linguistics.

Eneko Agirre, Oier López de Lacalle, and Aitor Soroa. 2014. Random Walks for Knowledge-based Word Sense Disambiguation. *Comput. Linguist.*, 40(1):57–84.

Amit Bagga and Breck Baldwin. 1998. Algorithms for Scoring Coreference Chains. In *The First International Conference on Language Resources and Evaluation Workshop on Linguistics Coreference*, pages 563–566, Granada, Spain.

Klara Ceberio, Itziar Aduriz, Arantza Díaz de Ilarraza, and Ines Garcia-Azkoaga. 2016. Coreferential relations in Basque: the annotation process. In *Theoretical Developments in Hispanic Linguistics*. The Ohio State University.

Pascal Denis and Jason Baldridge. 2009. Global Joint Models for Coreference Resolution and Named Entity Classification. *Procesamiento del Lenguaje Natural*, 43:87–96.

Greg Durrett and Dan Klein. 2013. Easy Victories and Uphill Battles in Coreference Resolution. In *Proceedings of the 2013 Conference on Empirical Methods in Natural Language Processing*, pages 1971–1982, Seattle, Washington, USA. Association for Computational Linguistics.

Greg Durrett and Dan Klein. 2014. A Joint Model for Entity Analysis: Coreference, Typing, and Linking. *TACL*, 2:477–490.

Christiane Fellbaum, editor. 1998. *WordNet: an electronic lexical database*. MIT Press.

Barbara A. Fox. 1993. *Discourse structure and anaphora: written and conversational English*. Cambridge Univeristy Press.

Hannaneh Hajishirzi, Leila Zilles, Daniel S. Weld, and Luke Zettlemoyer. 2013. Joint Coreference Resolution and Named-Entity Linking with Multi-Pass Sieves. In *Proceedings of the 2013 Conference on Empirical Methods in Natural Language Processing*, pages 289–299, Seattle, Washington, USA. Association for Computational Linguistics.

Jonathan K. Kummerfeld and Dan Klein. 2013. Error-Driven Analysis of Challenges in Coreference Resolution. In *Proceedings of the 2013 Conference on Empirical Methods in Natural Language Processing*, pages 265–277, Seattle, Washington, USA.

Heeyoung Lee, Angel Chang, Yves Peirsman, Nathanael Chambers, Mihai Surdeanu, and Dan Jurafsky. 2013. Deterministic Coreference Resolution Based on Entity-centric, Precision-ranked Rules. *Computational Linguistics*, 39(4):885–916.

Xiaoqiang Luo. 2005. On Coreference Resolution Performance Metrics. In *Proceedings of the Conference on Human Language Technology and Empirical Methods in Natural Language Processing*, HLT '05, pages 25–32, Vancouver, British Columbia, Canada. Association for Computational Linguistics.

Pablo Mendes, Max Jakob, and Christian Bizer. 2012. DBpedia: A Multilingual Cross-domain Knowledge Base. In *Proceedings of the Eight International Conference on Language Resources and Evaluation (LREC'12)*, Istanbul, Turkey. European Language Resources Association (ELRA).

Nafise Sadat Moosavi and Michael Strube. 2016. Which Coreference Evaluation Metric Do You Trust? A Proposal for a Link-based Entity Aware Metric. In *Proceedings of the 54th Annual Meeting of the Association for Computational Linguistics*, pages 632–642, Berlin, Germany. Association for Computational Linguistics.

Elisabete Pociello, Eneko Agirre, and Izaskun Aldezabal. 2011. Methodology and construction of the Basque WordNet. *Language Resources and Evaluation*, 45(2):121–142.

Simone Paolo Ponzetto and Michael Strube. 2006. Exploiting Semantic Role Labeling, WordNet and Wikipedia for Coreference Resolution. In *Proceedings of the Main Conference on Human Language Technology Conference of the North American Chapter of the Association of Computational Linguistics*, HLT-NAACL '06, pages 192–199. Association for Computational Linguistics.

Sameer Pradhan, Xiaoqiang Luo, Marta Recasens, Eduard Hovy, Vincent Ng, and Michael Strube. 2014. Scoring Coreference Partitions of Predicted Mentions: A Reference Implementation. In *Proceedings of the 52nd Annual Meeting of the Association for Computational Linguistics*, pages 30–35, Baltimore, Maryland. Association for Computational Linguistics.

Altaf Rahman and Vincent Ng. 2011. Coreference Resolution with World Knowledge. In *Proceedings of the 49th Annual Meeting of the Association for Computational Linguistics: Human Language Technologies*, HLT '11, pages 814–824, Portland, Oregon. Association for Computational Linguistics.

Lev Ratinov and Dan Roth. 2012. Learning-based Multi-sieve Co-reference Resolution with Knowledge. In *Proceedings of the 2012 Joint Conference on Empirical Methods in Natural Language Processing and Computational Natural Language Learning*, EMNLP-CoNLL '12, pages 1234–1244, Jeju Island, Korea. Association for Computational Linguistics.

Marta Recasens and Eduard Hovy. 2011. BLANC: Implementing the Rand index for coreference evaluation. *Natural Language Engineering*, 17(4):485–510.

Marta Recasens, Matthew Can, and Daniel Jurafsky. 2013. Same Referent, Different Words: Unsupervised Mining of Opaque Coreferent Mentions. In *Proceedings of the 2013 Conference of the North American Chapter of the Association for Computational Linguistics: Human Language Technologies*, pages 897–906, Atlanta, Georgia. Association for Computational Linguistics.

Ander Soraluze, Olatz Arregi, Xabier Arregi, and Arantza Díaz de Ilarraza. 2015. Coreference Resolution for Morphologically Rich Languages. Adaptation of the Stanford System to Basque. *Procesamiento del Lenguaje Natural*, 55:23–30.

Ander Soraluze, Olatz Arregi, Xabier Arregi, and Arantza Díaz De Ilarraza. 2016. Improving mention detection for Basque based on a deep error analysis. *Natural Language Engineering*, pages 1–34, 007.

Fabian M. Suchanek, Gjergji Kasneci, and Gerhard Weikum. 2007. YAGO: a core of semantic knowledge unifying WordNet and Wikipedia. In *Proceedings of the 16th International World Wide Web Conference (WWW 2007)*, pages 697–706.

Olga Uryupina, Massimo Poesio, Claudio Giuliano, and Kateryna Tymoshenko. 2011. Disambiguation and Filtering Methods in Using Web Knowledge for Coreference Resolution. In *FLAIRS Conference*, pages 317–322. AAAI Press.

Yannick Versley, Massimo Poesio, and Simone Ponzetto. 2016. Using Lexical and Encyclopedic Knowledge. In Massimo Poesio, Roland Stuckardt, and Yannick Versley, editors, *Anaphora Resolution: Algorithms, Resources, and Applications*, pages 393–429. Springer Berlin Heidelberg, Berlin, Heidelberg.

Marc Vilain, John Burger, John Aberdeen, Dennis Connolly, and Lynette Hirschman. 1995. A Model-theoretic Coreference Scoring Scheme. In *Proceedings of the 6th Conference on Message Understanding*, MUC6 '95, pages 45–52. Association for Computational Linguistics.

Improving Polish Mention Detection with Valency Dictionary

Maciej Ogrodniczuk
Institute of Computer Science
Polish Academy of Sciences
Jana Kazimierza 5
01-248 Warsaw, Poland
maciej.ogrodniczuk@ipipan.waw.pl

Bartłomiej Nitoń
Institute of Computer Science
Polish Academy of Sciences
Jana Kazimierza 5
01-248 Warsaw, Poland
bartek.niton@gmail.com

Abstract

This paper presents results of an experiment integrating information from valency dictionary of Polish into a mention detection system. Two types of information is acquired: positions of syntactic schemata for nominal and verbal constructs and secondary prepositions present in schemata. The syntactic schemata are used to prevent (for verbal realizations) or encourage (for nominal groups) constructing mentions from phrases filling multiple schema positions, the secondary prepositions – to filter out artificial mentions created from their nominal components. Mention detection is evaluated against the manual annotation of the Polish Coreference Corpus in two settings: taking into account only mention heads or exact borders.

1 Introduction

Coreference resolution systems are believed to suffer from lack of integration of "deeper" knowledge, with respect to both semantics and world knowledge, while it has been recognized from the very beginning (Hobbs, 1978) that they make very important and at the same time difficult factors in the process[1] and that present attempts of integration of such features are bringing only small improvements to the overall accuracy (see next section for examples). The slow progress in solving complex semantics- or knowledge-related issues we are experiencing today is promoting the switch into the search of new algorithms and models and probably also adds to the general loss of global interest in coreference resolution.

Nevertheless we argue that such situation should not be considered as failure of semantic approaches but rather as a consequence of enormous dimensions and complication of the knowledge system which needs to be applied to linguistic processing, including reference decoding. On the contrary, we believe that the method of small steps towards the big goal is constantly bringing useful models and resources to the field, year by year growing in size and complexity. It is particularly important for languages other than English where more subtle properties of semantic constructs can influence the results.

In the current paper we show how integration of a relatively simple rule taking into consideration verbal and nominal valency in Polish slightly but consequently improves mention detection scores.

2 Related Work

(Kehler et al., 2004) integrated preferences inferred from statistics of subject–verb, verb–object and possessive–noun predicate–argument frequencies into a pronoun-based resolution system which resulted in 1% accuracy improvement. Several works integrating semantic processing into coreference resolution were also proposed, e.g. (Ponzetto and Strube, 2006b) integrated predicate-argument pairs into (Soon et al., 2001)'s resolution system which yielded 1.5 MUC F_1 score improvement on ACE 2003 data.

(Ponzetto and Strube, 2006a; Ponzetto and Strube, 2007) used Wikipedia, WordNet and semantic role tagging to compute semantic relatedness between anaphor and antecedent to achieve 2.7 points MUC F_1 score improvement on ACE

[1]Cf. a concluding sentence from (Sapena et al., 2013): "Although it is clearly necessary to incorporate world knowledge to move forward in the field of coreference resolution, the process required to introduce such information in a constructive way has not yet been found." See also e.g. Michael Strube's presentation at CORBON 2016: "The (Non)Utility of Semantics for Coreference Resolution".

Proceedings of the 2nd Workshop on Coreference Resolution Beyond OntoNotes (CORBON 2017), co-located with EACL 2017, pages 17–23,
Valencia, Spain, April 4, 2017.

2003 data.

(Rahman and Ng, 2011) labelled nominal phrases with FrameNet semantic roles achieving 0.5 points B^3 and CEAF F_1 score improvement and used YAGO type and means relations achieving 0.7 to 2.8 points improvement on OntoNotes-2 and ACE 2004/2005 data.

(Durrett and Klein, 2013) incorporated in their system shallow semantics by using WordNet hypernymy and synonymy, number and gender data for nominals and propers, named entity types and latent clusters computer from English Gigaword corpus, reaching 1.6 points improvement on gold data and 0.36 points on system data.

For Polish, WordNet and Wikipedia-related features were used to improve verification of semantic compatibility for common nouns and named entities in BARTEK-3 coreference resolution system (Ogrodniczuk et al., 2015, Section 12.3) resulting in improvement of approx. 0.5 points MUC F_1 score. Experiments with integration of external vocabulary resources coming from websites registering the newest linguistic trends in Polish, fresh loan words and neologisms not yet covered by traditional dictionaries have been also performed showing low coverage of new constructs in evaluation data (Ogrodniczuk, 2013).

All these results showed challenges regarding knowledge-based resources, mainly concerning the memory and time complexity of the task as well as low coverage of complex features in the test data, but at the same time brought some (sometimes tiny) improvements to coreference resolution scores.

3 Problem Definition

In our approach *mentions* are defined as text fragments (nominal groups including attached prepositional phrases and relative clauses) which could potentially create references to discourse world objects. Such definition has both syntactic and semantic grounds: inclusion of extensive syntactically dependent phrases into mention borders is important due to semantic understanding of mentions: *pierwszy człowiek na Księżycu* 'the first man on the Moon' or *samochód, który potrącił moją żonę* 'the car which hit my wife' have different meanings than just *człowiek* 'the man' or *samochód* 'the car'. One of the consequences of this distinction is treating as mentions all embedded phrases with heads distinct from the head of the main phrase (meaning that they corresponded to different entities). Therefore, in the example:

(1) *szef działu firmy*
'the head of the branch of the company'

three noun phrases should be considered as mentions referring to, accordingly, 'the head of the branch of the company', 'the branch of the company' and 'the company' itself.

The need of exact mention border detection stands in contradiction with unavailability of a constituency parser for Polish with sufficient coverage[2] which could solve most of the attachment problems. Current state-of-the-art mention detector for Polish (see Section 4.3) identifies nominal groups with a relatively old Spejd shallow parser. Our work attempts to use valency schemata from a recently created valency dictionary for Polish (see Section 4.1) for two purposes: to prevent mention borders to cross positions of a syntactic schema and to filter out mentions created from nominal components of secondary prepositions, also present in the valency dictionary.

4 Resources and Tools

4.1 Walenty, a Polish Valence Dictionary

Walenty (Przepiórkowski et al., 2014)[3] is a comprehensive human- and machine-readable dictionary of Polish valency information for verbs, nouns, adjectives and adverbs. It consists of two interconnected layers, syntactic and semantic, and features precise linguistic description, including the structural case, clausal subjects, complex prepositions, comparative constructions, control and raising and semantically defined phrase types. Lexicon entries have strictly defined formal structure and the represented syntactic and semantic phenomena are always attested in linguistic reality, with the National Corpus of Polish (Przepiórkowski et al., 2012, later referred to as NKJP) as a primary source of data and Internet and linguistic literature as secondary sources.

Each lexical entry is identified by its lemma and consists of a number of syntactic valence schemata with each schema being a set of syntactic positions. Apart from the two labeled argument

[2]Currently available constituency parsers for Polish such as Świgra (`http://zil.ipipan.waw.pl/Świgra`) or POLFIE (`http://zil.ipipan.waw.pl/LFG`) do not yet guarantee sufficient coverage of natural language constructs.

[3]See also `http://walenty.ipipan.waw.pl/`.

Schema for:	łączyć			
Function:	subj	obj		
Phrase types:	np(str)	np(str)	np(inst)	prepnp(z,inst)

Figure 1: A sample schema in Walenty.

positions, subject and object, usual phrase types are considered, such as nominal phrases (NP), prepositional phrases (PREPNP), adjectival phrases (ADJP), clausal phrases (CP), etc. Phrase types can be further parameterised by corresponding grammatical categories, e.g., NP and ADJP are parameterised by information concerning case. The underscore symbol '_' denotes any value of a grammatical category, e.g., INFP(_) denotes infinitival phrase of any aspect.

Figure 1 presents a sample schema for the verb *łączyć* ('to link') with subject, object, nominal phrase in the instrumental case and prepositional phrase using preposition *z* ('with') and nominal component in the instrumental case again, as in the following example:

(2) *Potężne [komputery]*$_{\text{SUBJ}}$ *[łączą]*$_{\text{VERB}}$ *[firmę]*$_{\text{OBJ}}$ *[światłowodami]*$_{\text{NP(INST)}}$ *[z cyfrowym światem]*$_{\text{PREPNP(Z,INST)}}$.

'Powerful [computers]$_{\text{SUBJ}}$ [link]$_{\text{VERB}}$ [the company]$_{\text{OBJ}}$ [with the digital world]$_{\text{PREPNP(Z,INST)}}$ [using optical fiber]$_{\text{NP(INST)}}$.'

As of January 2017, Walenty contains over 65K schemata for 12K Polish verbs and 16K schemata for about 2500 nouns and is still expanding.

In our experiments we use Walenty in textual format (Hajnicz et al., 2015) which can be downloaded directly from Slowal Web application[4] (Nitoń et al., 2016). The version used in our experiment dates January 17, 2017.

4.2 Polish Coreference Corpus

The Polish Coreference Corpus[5] (Ogrodniczuk et al., 2015) is a large corpus of Polish general nominal coreference built upon NKJP. Each text of the corpus is a 250–350-word sample consisting of full subsequent paragraphs extracted from a larger text. With its 1900 documents from 14 text genres, containing about 540K tokens, 180K mentions and 128K coreference clusters, the PCC is among the largest manually annotated coreference corpora in the international community.

Mentions in PCC are understood as broadly as possible, with the following components included in the nominal phrase:

1. adjectives adjusting their form (case, number, gender) to the superordinate noun, e.g. *kolorowe kwiaty, duży czerwony tramwaj, lebiodka pospolita* 'colourful flowers', 'big red tram', 'oregano'
2. adjectives in genitive, singular, neuter, e.g. *coś fantastycznego, nic dziwnego* 'something fantastic', 'nothing strange'
3. nouns adjusting its case and number to the superordinate noun (apposition), e.g. *malarz pejzażysta, miasto Łódź* 'a landscape painter', 'the city of Łódź'
4. nouns in genitive, e.g. *kolega brata, protokół przesłuchania* 'a friend of my brother', 'the protocol of the hearing'
5. numeral phrases as subordinate elements of the nominal element, e.g. *zabójca pięciu kobiet* 'the killer of five women'
6. adjective participles adjusting its form to the superordinate noun, together with its subordinate element, e.g. *nadchodzące zmiany, rozbudowany hotel, zapaleńcy prowadzący swoje wojenki* 'oncoming changes', 'expanded hotel', 'hotheads waging their little wars'
7. relative clauses, e.g. *dziewczyna, o której rozmawiamy* 'the girl we talked about'
8. prepositional-nominal phrases, e.g. *ustawa o podatku dochodowym, droga na skróty* 'the law on income tax', 'a way across the country'
9. particles, e.g. *prawie cała rodzina, tylko ty* 'almost the whole family', 'only you'
10. adverbs as adjectives and participle modifiers, e.g. *szalenie ciekawy film* 'incredibly interesting film'.

[4]http://zil.ipipan.waw.pl/Slowal
[5]http://zil.ipipan.waw.pl/PCC

Similarly some phrases with syntactic head other than nominal were also considered mentions, such as numeral phrases or coordinated nominal phrases.

The current version of PCC data is 0.92 dated December 29, 2014.

4.3 Mention Detector for Polish

The state-of-the-art mention detection tool for Polish is MentionDetector[6] which uses information from morphosyntactic, shallow syntactic and named entity annotations created with state-of-the-art tools for Polish. MentionDetector is mostly a rule based tool with a statistical mechanism for detecting zero subjects. The following constructs are recognized:

1. single-segment nouns and nominal groups, detected with Spejd shallow parser[7] (Przepiórkowski and Buczyński, 2007) fitted with an adaptation of the NKJP grammar of Polish (Ogrodniczuk et al., 2014)

2. pronouns, identified with a disambiguating morphosyntactic tagger Pantera[8] (Acedański, 2010) with a morphological analyser and lemmatizer Morfeusz[9] (Woliński, 2014)

3. zero subjects, detected with a custom solution (Kopeć, 2014)

4. nominal named entities, detected with Nerf[10] (Waszczuk et al., 2013).

The current version of MentionDetector is 1.3 dated October 13, 2016.

5 The Experiment

The idea for the experiment is based on the observation that delimitation of mentions based on their semantic understanding is different for nominal and verbal constructs: for nominal phrases engaged in valency schemata (making the mention 'core') all syntactic positions should be included into the mention boundaries since they add vital supporting information to the core while for verbal phrases their nominal or prepositional positions correspond to different semantic roles and cannot be linked into a single mention. This assumption is verified with schemata acquired from Walenty against the PCC gold annotation.

The entry point for both nominal and verbal parts of the experiment is the same: finite verb forms as well as nominal and prepositional phrases are detected in the text[11] and matched against valency schemata. This is achieved by comparing base forms of syntactic heads of words to entries from the valency dictionary (directly for the main Walenty entry and by creating textual representations of phrase types for syntactic positions).

5.1 Nominal realizations

If a nominal schema with two positions corresponding to phrase types detected in the document is found, both the core nominal phrase and the dependent phrases are merged into a single mention, as in:

(3) *Od tamtego czasu miał miejsce [konflikt]*$_{\text{NOUN}}$ *[polskiego ambasadora]*$_{\text{NP(GEN)}}$ *[z polskim księdzem]*$_{\text{PREPNP(Z,INST)}}$.

'Since then there was [a conflict]$_{\text{NOUN}}$ [of the Polish ambassador]$_{\text{NP(GEN)}}$ [with the Polish priest]$_{\text{PREPNP(Z,INST)}}$.'

PREPNP constructions are created from the preposition word (tagged as PREP by Spejd) and the case of the head word from prepositional-nominal groups. NP constructions are created using the case of the nominal group head word.

The results of mention detection after adding this rule to base MentionDetector are presented in Table 1 under *Mention merging*.

5.2 Verbal realizations

If a verbal schema with nominal or prepositional positions is detected in the document, we prevent creation of a single mention out of phrases from different syntactic positions, cf.

(4) [Gratuluję]$_{\text{VERB}}$ [Włochom]$_{\text{NP(DAT)}}$ [awansu]$_{\text{NP(GEN)}}$.

'I [congratulate]$_{\text{VERB}}$ [the Italians]$_{\text{NP(DAT)}}$ [on their promotion]$_{\text{NP(GEN)}}$.'

[6] http://zil.ipipan.waw.pl/MentionDetector

[7] http://zil.ipipan.waw.pl/Spejd

[8] http://zil.ipipan.waw.pl/Pantera

[9] http://sgjp.pl/morfeusz/index.html.en

[10] http://zil.ipipan.waw.pl/Nerf

[11] In order to process prepositional phrases Spejd shallow grammar was adapted to detect prepositional-nominal groups (PREPNG).

The results of mention detection after adding this rule are presented in Table 1 under *Mention cleaning*, note that *nominal realizations* rule is also active.

5.3 Secondary Prepositions and Phraseological Compounds

Another valuable information present in Walenty is a list of approx. 200 secondary prepositions used in syntactic schemata[12]. Since secondary prepositions are lexicalized combinations of primary (monomorphemic) prepositions and nominal or prepositional phrases, their nominal components can be often automatically (and always incorrectly) marked as mentions. Table 1 under *Walenty list* presents the results of removal of such mentions from the system set.

The next step was expansion of the list of complex prepositions using other available sources, the first of them being *The PWN Universal Dictionary of the Polish Language*[13] (Dubisz, 2006). Secondly, rules responsible for building secondary prepositions out of individual prepositions and nouns in Spejd grammar were examined and their components were also excluded from the list of mention candidates. Last but not least, Spejd grammar rules for idiomatic expressions (marked as *frazeo*) were investigated to collect indeclinable phraseologic phrases with nominal component (underlined below) such as:

- particle-adverbs (`Qub`), e.g. *bez wątpienia* 'without a doubt'
- adverbs (`Adv`), e.g. *w lot* 'immediately'
- interjections (`Interj`), e.g. *broń Boże* 'heaven forbid'
- adjectives (`Adj`), e.g. *na poziomie* 'ambitious'
- conjunctions (`Conj`), e.g. *przy czym* 'at the same time'
- compounds (`Comp`), e.g. *w miarę jak (słuchali)* 'as (they listened)'

That means that sometimes complex prepositions text strings are not always used as a preposition and we must know the wider text context to distinguish whether they are truly complex prepositions or constructions bringing up mention into the discourse. Spade helps us in this distinction.

The results of mention detection after adding this rule are presented in Table 1 under *Secondary prepositions*, note that *nominal realizations* and *verbal realizations* rules are also active.

6 Results

Results of mention detection follow the procedure described in (Ogrodniczuk et al., 2015). Precision, recall and F-measure are calculated using Scoreference application from the Polish Coreference Toolset[14]. As compared to SemEval approach (Recasens et al., 2010) where systems were rewarded with 1 point for correct mentions boundaries, 0.5 points for boundaries within the gold NP including its head, 0 otherwise, in our evaluation we decided not to reward partial matches but to provide two alternative mention detection scores: EXACT boundary match and HEAD match.

Table 1 compares the results of exact mention detection to the best available mention detection results for Polish. The baseline for our verification is the newest result of evaluation of current version of MentionDetector on PCC test data[15].

Nominal realizations rule increases mention detection by over 1%. We believe that it could be increased even higher with larger dictionary. Our rule is using noun constraints only and by far there are only about 2500 nouns in Walenty. Fortunately Walenty is still expanding and further score improvement is a matter of time.

Verbal realizations rule is bringing very small mention detection score improvement, on the other hand it is highly precise.

Head only detection results are presented for comparison, as we can see they have slightly increased after using *secondary prepositions and phraseological compounds* rule. This is because during this step we have removed a lot of wrong single-segment mentions (consisting of heads only) which has noticeable and positive impact on HEAD mention detection precision.

[12]See `http://walenty.ipipan.waw.pl/rozwiniecia_typow_fraz/`.

[13]Electronic version: `http://usjp.pwn.pl/`

[14]See all tools at `http://zil.ipipan.waw.pl/PolishCoreferenceTools`.

[15]The results reported in (Ogrodniczuk et al., 2015, pp. 239–240) are even lower (66.79% precision, 67.21% recall and 61.00% F_1 score for EXACT borders) probably due to recent changes in MentionDetector related to progress in null subject detection.

Configuration	EXACT Precision	EXACT Recall	EXACT F_1	HEAD Precision	HEAD Recall	HEAD F_1
Baseline	67.07%	67.19%	67.13%	88.68%	**89.37%**	89.02%
Mention merging	68.34%	67.95%	68.15%	88.63%	88.74%	88.69%
Mention cleaning	68.35%	**67.96%**	68.16%	88.63%	88.74%	88.69%
Secondary prepositions	**69.59%**	67.85%	**68.71%**	**90.02%**	88.30%	**89.15%**

Table 1: Mention detection evaluation results

7 Conclusions

The presented experiment showed usefulness of valency schemata in the process of mention detection although the scale of improvement was relatively small. It should be attributed to several factors such as the limited size of the valency dictionary or sparsity of cases where valency rules can intervene (as opposed to 'general' cases).

The setting used only two most frequent types of phrases present in valency schemata, nominal and prepositional phrases, so one of the next steps could be analysis how other types of phrases intervene in the process of mention construction.

Even though the gains are far from being huge as compared to the progress introduced to the field in the recent years by adoption of new algorithms and architectures, experiments with integration of knowledge and semantics into the process seem worth pursuing, particularly for languages other than English for which they may offer fine-tuning of the language-independent solutions bringing slow but stable progress to results of linguistic analysis.

Acknowledgements

The work reported here was carried out within the research project financed by the Polish National Science Centre (contract number 2014/15/B/HS2/03435).

References

Szymon Acedański. 2010. A morphosyntactic brill tagger for inflectional languages. In Hrafn Loftsson, Eiríkur Rögnvaldsson, and Sigrún Helgadóttir, editors, *Advances in Natural Language Processing: 7th International Conference on NLP, IceTAL 2010, Reykjavik, Iceland, August 16-18, 2010*, pages 3–14, Berlin, Heidelberg. Springer Berlin Heidelberg.

Stanisław Dubisz, editor. 2006. *Uniwersalny słownik języka polskiego PWN*. Wydawnictwo Naukowe PWN. vol. 1–4.

Greg Durrett and Dan Klein. 2013. Easy victories and uphill battles in coreference resolution. In *Proceedings of the 2013 Conference on Empirical Methods in Natural Language Processing*, pages 1971–1982, Seattle, Washington, USA, October. Association for Computational Linguistics.

Elżbieta Hajnicz, Bartłomiej Nitoń, Agnieszka Patejuk, Adam Przepiórkowski, and Marcin Woliński. 2015. Internetowy słownik walencyjny języka polskiego oparty na danych korpusowych. *Prace Filologiczne*, LXV:95–110.

Jerry R. Hobbs. 1978. Resolving Pronoun References. *Lingua*, 44:311–338.

Andrew Kehler, Douglas Appelt, Lara Taylor, and Aleksandr Simma. 2004. The (Non)Utility of Predicate-Argument Frequencies for Pronoun Interpretation. In *Proceedings of 2004 North American chapter of the Association for Computational Linguistics annual meeting*, pages 289–296.

Mateusz Kopeć. 2014. Zero subject detection for Polish. In *Proceedings of the 14th Conference of the European Chapter of the Association for Computational Linguistics, volume 2: Short Papers*, pages 221–225, Gothenburg, Sweden. Association for Computational Linguistics.

Bartłomiej Nitoń, Tomasz Bartosiak, and Elżbieta Hajnicz. 2016. Accessing and Elaborating *Walenty* — a Valence Dictionary of Polish — via Internet Browser. In Nicoletta Calzolari, Khalid Choukri, Thierry Declerck, Marko Grobelnik, Bente Maegaard, Joseph Mariani, Asuncion Moreno, Jan Odijk, and Stelios Piperidis, editors, *Proceedings of the 10th International Conference on Language Resources and Evaluation (LREC 2016)*, pages 1352–1359, Portorož, Slovenia. ELRA, European Language Resources Association.

Maciej Ogrodniczuk, Alicja Wójcicka, Katarzyna Głowińska, and Mateusz Kopeć. 2014. Detection of Nested Mentions for Coreference Resolution in Polish. In Maciej Ogrodniczuk and Adam Przepiórkowski, editors, *Advances in Natural Language Processing: Proceedings of the 9th International Conference on NLP, PolTAL 2014*, volume 8686 of *Lecture Notes in Computer Science*, pages 270–277, Warsaw, Poland. Springer International Publishing.

Maciej Ogrodniczuk, Katarzyna Głowińska, Mateusz Kopeć, Agata Savary, and Magdalena Zawisławska. 2015. *Coreference in Polish: Annotation, Resolution and Evaluation.* Walter De Gruyter.

Maciej Ogrodniczuk. 2013. Discovery of common nominal facts for coreference resolution: Proof of concept. In R. Prasath and T. Kathirvalavakumar, editors, *Mining Intelligence and Knowledge Exploration (MIKE 2013)*, volume 8284 of *Lecture Notes in Artificial Intelligence*, pages 709–716. Springer-Verlag, Berlin, Heidelberg.

Simone Paolo Ponzetto and Michael Strube. 2006a. Exploiting Semantic Role Labeling, WordNet and Wikipedia for Coreference Resolution. In *Proceedings of the Human Language Technology Conference of the NAACL, Main Conference*, pages 192–199, New York City, USA, June. Association for Computational Linguistics.

Simone Paolo Ponzetto and Michael Strube. 2006b. Semantic Role Labeling for Coreference Resolution. In *Proceedings of the 11th Conference of the European Chapter of the Association for Computational Linguistics: Posters & Demonstrations*, EACL '06, pages 143–146, Stroudsburg, PA, USA. Association for Computational Linguistics.

Simone Paolo Ponzetto and Michael Strube. 2007. Knowledge Derived from Wikipedia for Computing Semantic Relatedness. *Journal of Artificial Intelligence Research*, 30(1):181–212.

Adam Przepiórkowski and Aleksander Buczyński. 2007. Spejd: Shallow Parsing and Disambiguation Engine. In Zygmunt Vetulani, editor, *Proceedings of the 3rd Language & Technology Conference*, pages 340–344, Poznań, Poland.

Adam Przepiórkowski, Mirosław Bańko, Rafał L. Górski, and Barbara Lewandowska-Tomaszczyk, editors. 2012. *Narodowy Korpus Języka Polskiego*. Wydawnictwo Naukowe PWN, Warsaw.

Adam Przepiórkowski, Elżbieta Hajnicz, Agnieszka Patejuk, Marcin Woliński, Filip Skwarski, and Marek Świdziński. 2014. Walenty: Towards a comprehensive valence dictionary of Polish. In Nicoletta Calzolari, Khalid Choukri, Thierry Declerck, Hrafn Loftsson, Bente Maegaard, Joseph Mariani, Asuncion Moreno, Jan Odijk, and Stelios Piperidis, editors, *Proceedings of the 9th International Conference on Language Resources and Evaluation (LREC 2014)*, pages 2785–2792, Reykjavík, Iceland. ELRA.

Altaf Rahman and Vincent Ng. 2011. Coreference Resolution with World Knowledge. In *Proceedings of the 49th Annual Meeting of the Association for Computational Linguistics: Human Language Technologies*, pages 814–824.

Marta Recasens, Lluís Màrquez, Emili Sapena, M. Antònia Martí, Mariona Taulé, Véronique Hoste, Massimo Poesio, and Yannick Versley. 2010. SemEval-2010 Task 1: Coreference Resolution in Multiple Languages. In *Proceedings of the 5th International Workshop on Semantic Evaluation*, pages 1–8, Stroudsburg, PA, USA. Association for Computational Linguistics.

Emili Sapena, Lluís Padró, and Jordi Turmo. 2013. A Constraint-based Hypergraph Partitioning Approach to Coreference Resolution. *Computational Linguistics*, 39(4):847–884.

Wee Meng Soon, Hwee Tou Ng, and Daniel Chung Yong Lim. 2001. A Machine Learning Approach to Coreference Resolution of Noun Phrases. *Computational Linguistics*, 27(4):521–544.

Jakub Waszczuk, Katarzyna Głowińska, Agata Savary, Adam Przepiórkowski, and Michał Lenart. 2013. Annotation tools for syntax and named entities in the National Corpus of Polish. *International Journal of Data Mining, Modelling and Management*, 5(2):103–122.

Marcin Woliński. 2014. Morfeusz Reloaded. In Nicoletta Calzolari, Khalid Choukri, Thierry Declerck, Hrafn Loftsson, Bente Maegaard, Joseph Mariani, Asuncion Moreno, Jan Odijk, and Stelios Piperidis, editors, *Proceedings of the 9th International Conference on Language Resources and Evaluation (LREC 2014)*, pages 1106–1111, Reykjavík, Iceland. European Language Resources Association.

A Google-Proof Collection of French Winograd Schemas

Pascal Amsili and **Olga Seminck**
Laboratoire de Linguistique Formelle
Université Paris Diderot & CNRS
amsili@linguist.univ-paris-diderot.fr
olga.seminck@cri-paris.org

Abstract

This article presents the first collection of French Winograd Schemas. Winograd Schemas form anaphora resolution problems that can only be resolved with extensive world knowledge. For this reason the Winograd Schema Challenge has been proposed as an alternative to the Turing Test. A very important feature of Winograd Schemas is that it should be impossible to resolve them with statistical information about word co-occurrences: they should be *Google-proof*. We propose a measure of Google-proofness based on Mutual Information, and demonstrate the method on our collection of French Winograd Schemas.

1 Introduction

1.1 Winograd Schemas

Anaphora resolution depends on many factors from different linguistic levels. For example, grammatical role, number, gender, syntactic structure, phonological stress, distance between the referent and the anaphor and world knowledge all play a role. However, in automatic systems for anaphora resolution, rich semantics (world knowledge) is not often used. State of the art systems on the coreference task (Clark and Manning, 2016; Wiseman et al., 2015, *i.a.*) rely mostly on grammatical features, string matching features and some lexical semantic information (e.g., WordNet (Miller, 1995), named entities, or distributional semantics).

Winograd Schemas[1], as proposed by Levesque et al. (2011), form a special anaphora resolution challenge, because they cannot be resolved without a reasoning about world knowledge. A Winograd Schema is formed with a sentence containing an anaphor, along with a question about its antecedent and two possible answers (1). The correct answer should be obvious for a human.

(1) Nicolas could not carry his son because he was too ⟨weak⟩. Who was too ⟨weak⟩?
R0 : Nicolas
R1 : his son

The first sentence contains a word or an expression (labeled *special*) which can be replaced by another word or expression (*alternate*) in such a way that the sentence still makes sense, but the right answer to the question changes. For example in (1) if the special word 'weak' is replaced by 'heavy' (both in the sentence and in the question), the correct answer to the question is no longer R0, but R1. This property ensures that nothing in the overall structure of the schema prevents any NP to function as a possible antecedent.

According to this definition, for each Winograd Schema we get in fact two (related) questions (that we also call *items* in the rest of this paper).

1.2 Google-Proofness

Levesque et al. (2011) underline that the type of knowledge needed to resolve Winograd Schemas could be characterized as *thinking*, or *reasoning* — see also Levesque (2014). The idea is that Winograd Schemas cannot be resolved with only grammatical, or statistical information, nor any other non-semantic feature often used in standard coreference resolution systems. So in particular, the schemas should not be resolvable by typing the question and the answers into a search engine, such as Google, or by doing any obvious statistic test on a corpus. This feature is called *Google-proofness*. For instance, the item (2) is probably not Google-proof, because it is imaginable that

[1]Winograd Schemas are named after the examples Winograd (1972) used to illustrate the difficulty of natural language understanding.

Proceedings of the 2nd Workshop on Coreference Resolution Beyond OntoNotes (CORBON 2017), co-located with EACL 2017, pages 24–29,
Valencia, Spain, April 4, 2017.

"Galaxies are spread all over the universe" gets more Google hits than *"Astronomers are spread all over the universe."*.

(2) [2]Many astronomers are engaged in the search for distant galaxies. They are spread all over the ⟨universe⟩. What are spread all over the ⟨universe⟩?
R0 : the astronomers
R1 : the galaxies

On the other hand, for humans, Winograd Schemas should be obvious to resolve. Consequently, human performance should be near 100%. Indeed, Bender (2015) found a 92% success rate for humans on the English collection.

1.3 Test for Artificial Intelligence

Winograd Schemas can be seen as a difficult test of artificial intelligence. Indeed, Levesque et al. (2011) proposed the Winograd Schema Challenge (WSC) as an alternative to the Turing Test (Turing, 1950) —according to which a successful artificial intelligence system should be able to convince a human judge that it is human by conversing with him or her. In addition to the fact that resolving Winograd Schemas requires sophisticated reasoning, Levesque et al. (2011) argue that they overcome two majors issues of the Turing test. The first issue is that in order to pass the Turing test, a computer has to pretend to be human, in order to give human-like answers to questions like "How old are you?" or "Do you like chocolate?". The capacity to imitate a human behavior is in this respect orthogonal to the question of intelligence. The second issue of the Turing Test is the format of free conversation, which allows a system to use strategies to avoid answering difficult questions, for example by changing the subject, or making a joke. Winograd Schemas on the other hand, force the system to answer and do not allow evasive behavior.

1.4 State of the Art

In 2016 the first Winograd Schema Challenge was organized (Morgenstern et al., 2016). The task consisted of a pronoun disambiguation problem inspired by the format of Winograd Schemas.

Liu et al. (2016) submitted the winning system. It was based on unsupervised learning upon common sense knowledge bases and performed at a 58% success rate. After the WSC took place, the same group elaborated their system further, so that it was able to even attain a 66.7% success rate. It should be noted that the items that were used for the challenge were slightly different from the schemas that we have presented above: the items were not built in pairs through a common schema, and there were sometimes more than two antecedent candidates (3). As a consequence the baseline (chance level) for pronoun disambiguation problems was lower than 50% : 45% according to Liu et al. (2016).

(3) Mrs. March gave the mother tea and gruel, while she dressed the little baby as tenderly as if it had been her own.
As if <u>it</u> had been: tea / gruel / baby

Whereas the state of the art established by Liu et al. (2016) is much higher than the baseline, the result is still very far from the near 100% expected human score. Other systems that were not submitted to the competition can be found in literature; they often concentrate on a subset of schemas for which they developed a strategy for which we don't know how well it would generalize to the complete collection (Bailey et al., 2015; Schüller, 2014; Sharma et al., 2015, *i.a.*).

1.5 Our Contribution

Since the anaphora in the WSC can only be resolved with world knowledge, working on Winograd Schemas is an excellent way to develop models with rich semantic representations. We decided to provide a first collection of French schemas to encourage the development of these types of model for the French language. Having a French collection of schemas also enables more cross-linguistic comparison. Today there is a collection of 144 schemas for English that has been entirely translated into Japanese and 12 of the English schemas have also been translated into Chinese[3], but no documentation about the translation/adaptation method is provided. Our collection is also translated (or, rather, adapted) from the English set. We will say a few words about the adaptation process below.

While working on the adaptation of the English set, we also wanted to take seriously the constraint that Winograd Schemas should be Google-proof and therefore checked that our schemas were not

[2]taken from `http://www.cs.nyu.edu/faculty/davise/papers/WinogradSchemas/WSfailed.html`

[3]These collections can be found on `http://www.cs.nyu.edu/faculty/davise/papers/WinogradSchemas/WS.html`

(too) sensitive to simple statistical information. We developed a simple method that uses corpus statistics to see if one of the two answers is more likely to be the correct one. We show that our method is not able to get a good score on the collection of schemas as a whole, even though certain items are more sensitive to statistics than others and if carefully selected, could rise the theoretical baseline score of 50% by 4 to 5 %.

2 Collection of French Schemas

Our collection contains 107 Winograd Schemas, which yields 214 questions. We based our set of French Winograd Schemas on the English collection of Levesque et al. (2011). We started by trying to translate the English version. This was challenging, because the schemas are only valid if they contain an anaphor with the same number and gender as the two possible answers. For example, for an item like (4), we cannot use a direct translation, as the word 'hair' in French (*cheveux*) is plural, while 'drain' (*siphon*) is singular.

(4) The drain is clogged with hair. It has to be [cleaned/removed].

If the straightforward translation was not available, we tried to find another word that met the gender and number criteria, for example in (4) we replaced 'hair' with 'soap' (*savon*).

A second problem was that a literal translation could make one of the two versions of the schema ambiguous. Consider (5) with the alternate word ⟨indiscreet⟩. The French translation for 'indiscreet' is *indiscrète*. It turns out that in French *une personne indiscrète* — besides a person that reveals things that should stay secret — can also be somebody who *tries insistently to find out what should stay secret*, that is, a nosy person. In the French version of (5) we therefore changed the alternate to ⟨bavarde⟩ *(talkative)*.

(5) Susan knows all about Ann's personal problems because she is [nosy/indiscreet].

We always privileged the most natural sounding solution and avoided long translations. Every item had to be validated by three native speakers of French. First, two interns translated the English schemas into French. Second, a third intern validated and improved the collection. And in the end, the entire collection was validated by the authors. Items that we could not find a solution for were excluded from our final set.

All our 107 Winograd Schemas can be freely downloaded from the following webpage: `http://www.llf.cnrs.fr/winograd-fr`. Every schema has a reference to the English schema it was translated from or inspired by.

3 Test of Google-Proofness

By Google-proofness we understand that there should be no obvious statistical test over text corpora that will reliably disambiguate the anaphor of an item correctly (Levesque et al., 2011).

Although we translated our schemas from the English collection of Levesque et al. (2011) that were at least partially checked to be Google-proof, we wanted to investigate further if obvious statistics does not help to solve our items. We therefore defined a simple statistic test based on Mutual Information.

3.1 Mutual Information

Mutual Information is a concept from Information Theory (Shannon and Weaver, 1949) that measures the mutual dependence of two random variables. Mutual Information can be used to measure word association: when two words x and y are mutually dependent, the probability of their cooccurrence $P(x, y)$ will be higher than the probability of observing them together by chance : $MI(x, y)$ will be positive (equation 1). (Ward Church and Hanks, 1990)

$$MI(x, y) = log_2 \left(\frac{P(x, y)}{P(x)P(y)} \right) \quad (1)$$

To test the Google-proofness of our schemas, for each question we measured the Mutual Information between the lexemes of the answers and the special, or the alternate. For example in the first item of (6), we measured *MI* between *sculpture* and *encombrer* and *étagère* and *encombrer* (7).

(6) La sculpture est tombée de l'étagère car elle était trop [encombrée/lourde].
Qu'est-ce qui était trop [encombré/lourd]?
R0 : la sculpture
R1 : l'étagère
The sculpture fell off the shelf because it was too [cluttered/heavy].
What was too [cluttered/heavy]?
R0 : the sculpture
R1 : the shelf

(7) *MI(sculpture, encombrer)* = 4.23
MI(étagère, encombrer) = 10.01

The simplest way to exploit these scores is to choose the answer which maximizes *MI* scores, so here for instance R1, which turns out to be the correct answer. However, the difference between the two scores, which ranges from .01 to around 10 in our data set, is likely to be, in some cases, too small to be reliable.

Therefore we introduce various thresholds of minimal difference between *MI* scores. We vary the threshold from 0 to 4 and observe the impact on accuracy.

3.2 Applicability of the measure

It should be noted that many items, in the original set as well as in ours, have proper nouns as possible answers (8). This in itself should ensure Google-proofness since cooccurrence frequencies of proper nouns with lexical nouns is likely to be random. In our set 44 schemas are of this sort, but we have decided to include them in the scores.

(8) [4]Steve follows Fred's example in everything. He [admires/influences] him hugely. Who [admires/ influences] whom?

An important aspect of our method is that it requires that there be a way to extract the words between which *MI* is to be computed. This method is in fact based on the comparison between the two possible answers. For instance, with (6), the two possible full answers for the question formed with the special word are:

- the sculpture was too cluttered (R0, special)
- the shelf was too cluttered (R1, special)

while the two possible answers for the question formed with the alternate word are:

- the sculpture was too heavy (R0, alternate)
- the shelf was too heavy (R1, alternate)

In such a case, it is obvious to find the pairs of words for which we want to compute *MI*.

However, some schemas do not offer the same possibility. Consider (9). In this case, since the answers do not include the special/alternate word, the pair of possible answers is exactly the same for both questions derived from this schema. So any *MI* score that could be computed are going to be the same for both questions, to which the correct answers are by construction different. We haven't included the 30 items of this sort in our scores.

[4]taken from `http://www.cs.nyu.edu/faculty/davise/papers/WinogradSchemas/WS.html`

(9) In the middle of the outdoor concert, the rain started falling, [and/but] it continued until 10. What continued until 10?
R0 : The rain
R1 : the concert

We have 107 schemas in our collection, which yields 214 questions. 30 items were removed for the reasons we have just exposed, and 2 more schemas were removed because the possible answers R0 and R1 comprise the special/alternate words. All together, we measured Mutual Information for 90 schemas (180 items).

3.3 Probability Estimation

To estimate Mutual Information we used unsmoothed frequency counts from FrWaC, the French version of Web as a Corpus (Baroni et al., 2009), which is a corpus of 1.6 billion tokens from the `.fr` domain of the Internet. If the answers, the special, or the alternate were formed by multiple words, we took the frequency counts of the lexical head. Except in a few special cases, we measured the frequencies of lemmas rather than word-forms. We used a fixed corpus and not the Google search engine because the counts on Google are not stable in time and also optimization algorithms could alter the counts (Lapata and Keller, 2005).

3.4 Results

In Table 1 we can see the accuracy of the statistical method based on *MI* for different thresholds of difference in the scores of the two answers. Out of the 180 items we considered, 49 items could not get a score, because either one of the words did not appear at all or the coocurrence was not found in the corpus.

One should keep in mind that answering at random would give an accuracy around 50%. So the accuracy we get when no threshold is applied (55%) is clearly not satisfactory, and suggests, as we expected, that using any difference in *MI* scores is very similar to answering at random. The accuracy score reaches 70% however for a threshold of Δ 2.5, which is much better, but then the number of items to which the method applies is drastically small, namely less than 15% of the items.

The curves on Figure 1 plot accuracy and coverage as given in Table 1, along with another measure, that we call success rate. It is the theoretical accuracy that we would get by answering at random for items for which the *MI* difference is be-

Threshold	# Items	Accuracy	Coverage
None	131	0.55	0.40
Δ 0.5	95	0.59	0.31
Δ 1.0	73	0.62	0.25
Δ 1.5	59	0.64	0.21
Δ 2.0	38	0.68	0.14
Δ 2.5	30	0.70	0.12
Δ 3.0	25	0.68	0.09
Δ 3.5	18	0.67	0.07
Δ 4.0	15	0.60	0.05

Table 1: Results of the statistical method based on Mutual Information. Different thresholds give the minimal difference between the scores $I(R0, special)$ and $I(R1, special)$ that should be attained before the system can answer. '# Items' indicates the number of items that the method could answer to. 'Accuracy' is the accuracy of the method on the items that could be answered. 'Coverage' gives the accuracy on the 180 items we tried to solve with Mutual Information; if the method did not respond due to lack of counts or too high a threshold, this was counted as an error.

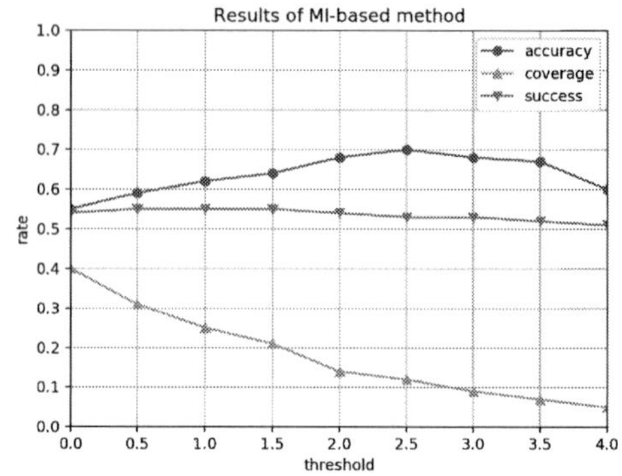

Figure 1: Results of the statistical methods based on Mutual Information. 'Accuracy' is the number of correct answers for the questions for which the method applies, while 'coverage' corresponds to the number of correct answers divided by the total number of questions. 'Success' is the theoretical success rate that would obtain a strategy consisting in using mutual information for the questions for which the Δ is over the threshold, and replying by chance for the other questions.

low the threshold, and using the *MI* difference for items for which it is above the threshold. We can see that this success rate never goes over 55%.

3.5 Discussion

Our collection as a whole seems to be Google-proof. Using Mutual Information as a strategy to resolve the schemas, we could not exceed a score of 55% success rate on the entire corpus, whichever threshold we used. However, there are a few cases where Mutual Information can be helpful (when the difference is high enough), which might still bring an improvement to a WSC system and one can easily imagine more sophisticated methods that would do better.

However, we would like to underline that we chose specifically not to use a sophisticated method. According to the concept of Google-proofness, Winograd Schemas should not be resolvable by obvious statistics. This raises the question where the boundary between obvious and smart statistics lies. For example, can we consider that a method such as word2vec (Mikolov et al., 2013) falls into the category of obvious statistics? Because we are not sure, we do not make the claim that the collection would resist any statistical test. But we are confident that it resists statistical test of the same level of simplicity as our mutual information measure.

4 Conclusion

Winograd Schemas, often referred to as a *new* Turing test, form an interesting AI problem. The schemas represent anaphora resolution problems that can only be resolved by rich semantic representations. To encourage research on the problems Winograd Schemas pose, we developed the first French Winograd Schema Collection. We investigated if our schemas could resist an obvious statistical method of resolution based on Mutual Information. It appeared that our collection is robust: only a small gain of 4 to 5% could be obtained by using the method.

Acknowledgments

We thank Sarah Ghumundee, Biljana Knežević, and Nicolas Bénichou who helped us prepare the items and compute mutual information scores. We also thank the three anonymous reviewers of the CORBON workshop for their feedback on our article. This work was supported in part by the École Doctorale Frontières du Vivant — Programme Bettencourt.

References

Dan Bailey, Amelia Harrison, Yuliya Lierler, Vladimir Lifschitz, and Julian Michael. 2015. The winograd schema challenge and reasoning about correlation. In *In Working Notes of the Symposium on Logical Formalizations of Commonsense Reasoning*.

Marco Baroni, Silvia Bernardini, Adriano Ferraresi, and Eros Zanchetta. 2009. The wacky wide web: a collection of very large linguistically processed web-crawled corpora. *Language resources and evaluation*, 43(3):209–226.

David Bender. 2015. Establishing a human baseline for the winograd schema challenge. In *MAICS*, pages 39–45.

Kevin Clark and D. Christopher Manning. 2016. Improving coreference resolution by learning entity-level distributed representations. In *Proceedings of the 54th Annual Meeting of the Association for Computational Linguistics (Volume 1: Long Papers)*, pages 643–653. Association for Computational Linguistics.

Mirella Lapata and Frank Keller. 2005. Web-based models for natural language processing. *ACM Transactions on Speech and Language Processing (TSLP)*, 2(1):3.

Hector J. Levesque, Ernest Davis, and Leora Morgenstern. 2011. The winograd schema challenge. In *AAAI Spring Symposium: Logical Formalizations of Commonsense Reasoning*, volume 46, page 47.

Hector J. Levesque. 2014. On our best behaviour. *Artificial Intelligence*, 212:27–35.

Quan Liu, Hui Jiang, Zhen-Hua Ling, Xiaodan Zhu, Si Wei, and Yu Hu. 2016. Combing context and commonsense knowledge through neural networks for solving winograd schema problems. *arXiv preprint arXiv:1611.04146*.

Tomas Mikolov, Ilya Sutskever, Kai Chen, Greg S. Corrado, and Jeff Dean. 2013. Distributed representations of words and phrases and their compositionality. In *Advances in neural information processing systems*, pages 3111–3119.

George A. Miller. 1995. Wordnet: a lexical database for english. *Communications of the ACM*, 38(11):39–41.

Leora Morgenstern, Ernest Davis, and Charles L. Ortiz Jr. 2016. Planning, executing, and evaluating the winograd schema challenge. *AI Magazine*, 37(1):50–54.

Peter Schüller. 2014. Tackling winograd schemas by formalizing relevance theory in knowledge graphs. In *Fourteenth International Conference on the Principles of Knowledge Representation and Reasoning*.

Claude E. Shannon and Warren Weaver. 1949. The mathematical theory of information.

Arpit Sharma, Nguyen H. Vo, Somak Aditya, and Chitta Baral. 2015. Towards addressing the winograd schema challenge-building and using a semantic parser and a knowledge hunting module. In *Proceedings of Twenty-Fourth International Joint Conference on Artificial Intelligence. AAAI*.

Alan M. Turing. 1950. Computing machinery and intelligence. *Mind*, 59(236):433–460.

Kenneth Ward Church and Patrick Hanks. 1990. Word association norms mutual information, and lexicography. *Computational Linguistics, Volume 16, Number 1, March 1990*.

Terry Winograd. 1972. Understanding natural language. *Cognitive psychology*, 3(1):1–191.

Sam Wiseman, M. Alexander Rush, Stuart Shieber, and Jason Weston. 2015. Learning anaphoricity and antecedent ranking features for coreference resolution. In *Proceedings of the 53rd Annual Meeting of the Association for Computational Linguistics and the 7th International Joint Conference on Natural Language Processing (Volume 1: Long Papers)*, pages 1416–1426. Association for Computational Linguistics.

Using Coreference Links to Improve Spanish-to-English Machine Translation

Lesly Miculicich Werlen and **Andrei Popescu-Belis**
Idiap Research Institute
Rue Marconi 19, CP 592
1920 Martigny, Switzerland
{lmiculicich,apbelis}@idiap.ch

Abstract

In this paper, we present a proof-of-concept of a coreference-aware decoder for document-level machine translation. We consider that better translations should have coreference links that are closer to those in the source text, and implement this criterion in two ways. First, we define a similarity measure between source and target coreference structures, by projecting the target ones onto the source ones, and then reusing existing monolingual coreference metrics. Based on this similarity measure, we re-rank the translation hypotheses of a baseline MT system for each sentence. Alternatively, to address the lack of diversity of mentions among the MT hypotheses, we focus on mention pairs and integrate their coreference scores with MT ones, resulting in post-editing decisions. Experiments with Spanish-to-English MT on the AnCora-ES corpus show that our second approach yields a substantial increase in the accuracy of pronoun translation, while BLEU scores remain constant.

1 Introduction

Considering entire texts for machine translation, rather than separate sentences, has the potential to improve the consistency of the translations. In this paper, we focus on coreference links, which connect referring expressions that denote the same entity within or across sentences. As perfect translations should provide the reader the same understanding of entities as the source texts, we propose to use the similarity of coreference links between a source text and its translation as a criterion to improve translation hypotheses. This information should be beneficial to the translation of pronouns, which often depends on the properties of their antecedent, but should also ensure lexical consistency in the translation of coreferent nouns.

We provide here the first proof-of-concept showing that the coreference criterion can lead to measurable improvements in the translation of referring expressions, in the case of Spanish-to-English machine translation (MT). To implement this criterion, we need to compute first the coreference links in the source and target texts. Then, we propose and compare two approaches: either computing a global coreference score by comparing the links and using it to rerank the hypotheses of an MT system; or integrating mention-pair scores from a coreference resolution system with MT scores, and post-editing each mention to maximize the total score.

The paper is organized as follows. In Section 2, we present an overview of related work on coreference and anaphora resolution and MT. In Section 3, we explain how we compute source and target-side coreference links, respectively by taking advantage of gold standard coreference links on the Spanish AnCora-ES corpus, and using the Stanford Coreference Resolution system on the English MT output – for both coreference-aware MT methods that we present. In Section 4, we compare coreference links globally by projecting the referring expressions (mentions) from target to source texts, and measuring similarity with existing coreference resolution metrics (MUC, B3, CEAF). As a sanity check, in Section 4.2, we show that better translations, in the sense of higher BLEU scores, exhibit higher coreference similarity scores as well. Global coreference similarity is then used in Section 4.3 as a constraint to rerank hypotheses of the Moses MT decoder. Alternatively, as the top MT hypotheses do not vary enough in terms of mentions, we propose in Section 5 a different method, which focuses only on

Proceedings of the 2nd Workshop on Coreference Resolution Beyond OntoNotes (CORBON 2017), co-located with EACL 2017, pages 30–40,
Valencia, Spain, April 4, 2017.

the translation variants of the mentions, and post-edits them using information from coreference chains in the source text. Finally, the results presented in Section 6 show that the second method increases the accuracy of pronoun translation from Spanish to English, while obtaining BLEU scores similar to those of the MT baseline.

2 Related Work

2.1 Coreference Resolution and Evaluation

Coreference resolution is the task of grouping together the expressions that refer to the same entity in a text. This task includes two stages: mention identification, and coreference resolution. The first stage is usually based on part-of-speech annotation and named-entity recognition. Candidate mentions are usually noun phrases, pronouns, and named entities (Lee et al., 2011). Coreference resolvers follow three main approaches: pairwise, re-ranking, and clustering. Pairwise resolvers perform a binary classification, predicting if two mentions refer to the same entity or not. This assumes strong independence of mentions and does not utilize features of the entire entity (Bengtson and Roth, 2008). The second approach lists a set of candidate antecedents for each mention that are simultaneously considered to find the best match. Interpolation between the best and worse candidate is considered (Wiseman et al., 2015; Bengtson and Roth, 2008). Finally, the clustering approach considers the features of a complete cluster of mentions to decide whether a mention belongs or not to a cluster (Clark and Manning, 2015; Fernandes et al., 2012).

Coreference resolution is typically evaluated in comparison with a gold-standard annotation (Popescu-Belis, 1999; Recasens and Hovy, 2011). The main metrics used for evaluation are MUC (Vilain et al., 1995), which counts the minimum number of links between mentions to be inserted or deleted in order to map the evaluated document to the gold-standard. The B^3 measure (Bagga and Baldwin, 1998) computes precision and recall for all mentions of a document, while CEAF (Luo, 2005) computes them at the entity level. BLANC (Recasens and Hovy, 2011) makes use of the Rand Index, an algorithm for the evaluation of clustering. These metrics are implemented in the scorer for CoNLL 2012 (Pradhan et al., 2014) and the SemEval 2013 one (Màrquez et al., 2013).

2.2 Coreference-Aware Machine Translation

Despite the numerous coreference and anaphora resolution systems designed in the past decades (Mitkov, 2002; Ng, 2010), the interest in using them to improve pronoun translation has only recently emerged (Le Nagard and Koehn, 2010; Hardmeier and Federico, 2010; Guillou, 2012). The still limited accuracy of coreference resolution may explain its restricted use in MT, although, it has long been known that some pronouns require knowledge of the antecedent for correct translation. For instance, Le Nagard and Koehn (2010) trained an English-French translation model on an annotated corpus in which each occurrence of the English pronouns *it* and *they* was annotated with the gender of its antecedent on the target side. Their system correctly translated 40 pronouns out of the 59 that they examined, but did not outperform the MT baseline. Recently, a model for MT decoding proposed by Luong (2016; 2017) combined several features of the antecedent candidates (gender, number and humanness) with an MT decoder, in a probabilistic way, and demonstrated improvement on pronouns.

Two shared tasks on pronoun-focused translation have been recently organized. The improvement of pronoun translation was only marginal with respect to a baseline SMT system in the 2015 shared task (Hardmeier et al., 2015), while the 2016 shared task was only aiming at pronoun prediction given source texts and lemmatized reference translations (Guillou et al., 2016). Some of the best systems developed for these tasks avoided, in fact, the direct use of anaphora resolution (with the exception of Luong et al. (2015)). For example, Callin et al. (2015) designed a classifier based on a feed-forward neural network, which considered as features the preceding nouns and determiners along with their part-of-speech tags. The winning systems of the 2016 task used deep neural networks: Luotolahti et al. (2016) and Dabre et al. (2016) summarized the preceding and following contexts of the pronoun to predict and passed them to a recurrent neural network. To the best of our knowledge, we present here the first proof-of-concept that coreference links across noun phrases and pronouns can serve to improve statistical MT.

3 Coreference Resolution for MT

A principle of translation is that the information conveyed in a document should be preserved in

Source	Human Translation	Machine Translation
La película narra la historia de [un joven parisiense]$_{c1}$ que marcha a Rumanía en busca de [una cantante zíngara]$_{c2}$, ya que [su]$_{c1}$ fallecido padre escuchaba siempre [sus]$_{c2}$ canciones.	The film tells the story of [a young Parisian]$_{c1}$ who goes to Romania in search of [a gypsy singer]$_{c2}$, as [his]$_{c1}$ deceased father use to listen to [her]$_{c2}$ songs.	The film tells the story of [a young Parisian]$_{c1}$ who goes to Romania in search of [a gypsy singer]$_{c2}$, as [his]$_{c2}$ deceased father always listened to [his]$_{c2}$ songs.
Pudiera considerarse un viaje fallido, porque [$\emptyset$]$_{c1}$ no encuentra [su]$_{c1}$ objetivo, pero el azar [le]$_{c1}$ conduce a una pequea comunidad...	It could be considered a failed journey, because [he]$_{c1}$ does not find [his]$_{c1}$ objective, but the fate leads [him]$_{c1}$ to a small community...	It could be considered [a failed trip]$_{c3}$, because [it]$_{c3}$ does not find [its]$_{c3}$ objective, but the chance leads $\emptyset$ to a small community...

Table 1: Comparison of coreference chains in the Spanish source vs. English human and machine translations. English chains were obtained with the Stanford coreference resolver (Manning et al., 2014). The chains are numbed $c_1, c_2, \ldots$ and are also color-coded. The void symbol $\emptyset$ indicates a correct null subject pronoun in Spanish, and an incorrect object pronoun dropped by the MT system. The third coreference chain (c_3) in the MT output is erroneous.

its translation. Here, we focus on the referential information, i.e. the coreference links between mentions. If we apply coreference resolution to a source text and to a faithful translation of it, then the grouping of mentions should be identical. We thus formulate the following criterion for MT: *better translations should have coreference links that are more similar to the source.*

Table 1 illustrates the above criterion on an example of Spanish-to-English translation, extracted from the AnCora-ES corpus (Recasens and Martí, 2010),[1] with source coreference chains coming from the AnCora-ES annotations. The automatic translation comes from a commercial online MT system, while the human translation was done by the authors of this paper. The Stanford Statistical Coreference Resolution system (Clark and Manning, 2015)[2] was applied to both translations, and the resulting coreference chains are indicated in the table with numbers and colors. We observe that the chains in the human translation match well those in the source, but this is less the case for the automatic translation, in particular due to wrong pronoun translations. Although the MT output is still understandable, this requires more time than with the human translation, due to the wrong set of coreference links inferred by the reader.

In what follows, we will implement a proof-of-concept coreference-aware MT system for Spanish-to-English translation. This pair is particularly challenging because Spanish is a pro-drop language, so that an MT system must not only select the correct translation of pronouns, but it must also generate English pronouns from Spanish null ones. In this study, in order to avoid introducing errors made by the coreference resolution system, we will always use on the source side the gold-standard coreference annotation from AnCora-ES (Recasens and Martí, 2010), which was used in the SemEval-2010 Task 1 on coreference resolution in multiple languages (Recasens et al., 2010).[3] As our proposal does not require specific training on coreference-annotated data, AnCora-ES will be used for testing only.

On the target side, as coreference resolution must be performed for each translation hypothesis, we must use an automatic system. One advantage of the Spanish-to-English direction is that English coreference resolution systems have been studied and developed for a long time, more than any other language, thus keeping coreference errors to a minimum. We use again the Stanford Statistical Coreference Resolution system proposed by Clark and Manning (2015). Moreover, to obtain pairwise mention scores, needed in Section 5, we use the code of the pairwise classifier available with the source code of the Stanford CoreNLP toolkit (Manning et al., 2014)[4].

[1] `http://clic.ub.edu/corpus/`

[2] `http://stanfordnlp.github.io/CoreNLP/coref.html`

[3] `http://stel.ub.edu/semeval2010-coref/`

[4] Source class 'edu.stanford.nlp.scoref.PairwiseModel' at `http://stanfordnlp.github.io/CoreNLP/`.

4 Using Coreference Similarity to Rerank MT Hypotheses

4.1 Measuring Coreference Similarity

After applying coreference resolution to the source and a candidate translation, we need to compare the sets of coreference links, with the source playing the role of the ground-truth or gold-standard. Traditional metrics for evaluating coreference resolution could be used, but they have been designed to compare texts in the same language, and not across different languages, which raises difficulties for matching the referring expressions (i.e. mentions, or markables).

We propose to project the mentions of the target text back to the source text, so that each word in the source is aligned with its corresponding translation (one or more words). This alignment can be obtained directly from the Moses MT system (see start of Section 4.3).

There is not always a one-to-one word correspondence between the words in the source and target sentences, and word order also differs. Thus, we apply the following heuristic to improve the cross-language mapping of the mentions. As through word-alignment the words that comprise the mentions may have changed order in the translation, we take the first and last words in the target side, aligned to any word of the mention in the source, and we assume that all words in between are also part of the mention. The null pronouns are transfer to the next immediate verb, and we refine the alignment to be sure these verbs are aligned to the generated pronoun in the target.

Once the target mentions are mapped to the source, we apply the MUC, B^3 and CEAF-m coreference similarity metrics from the CoNLL 2012 scorer (see Section 2.1) between the source document d_s and the projected target one d_t. To mitigate individual variations, we use the average of the three scores at the similarity criterion and note it $C_{sim}(d_t, d_s)$. We did not include BLANC in this pool based on initial experiments that showed that its rate of variation was much higher than the other three metrics.

4.2 Validating the Relationship between Coreference and Translation Quality

To validate the insight that better translations correlate with better coreference similarity scores, we present in Table 2 the MUC, B^3 and CEAF scores of a human translation vs. two systems: the Moses baseline phrase-based MT system used below and an online commercial MT system using neural networks. The source is a set of documents with ca. 3.5 thousand words with gold-standard coreference annotation from AnCora-ES. The English translation was done by the authors of the paper. On the target side, we applied the Stanford automatic coreference resolution system (Manning et al., 2014).

By definition, the best translation is made by the human. Then, according BLEU score measured on the same set of documents, the second best translation is made by the commercial MT with 49.4, and the last one by the baseline MT with 43.7. We observe that the coreference scores also decrease in this order, and they decrease consistently for the three evaluation metrics. These results thus support the principle that translation quality and coreference similarity are correlated. We will now show how to use this principle to improve translation quality.

Metric	Translation	Recall	Prec.	F1
MUC	Human	31	46	37
	Commercial MT	21	38	28
	Baseline MT	18	33	23
B^3	Human	24	49	32
	Commercial MT	20	38	26
	Baseline MT	17	40	24
CEAF	Human	41	40	41
	Commercial MT	34	39	36
	Baseline MT	32	35	33

Table 2: Coreference similarity scores (%) between source and target texts for different translations. The scores increase with the quality of translations.

4.3 Reranking MT Hypotheses

We propose to use the document-level coreference similarity score C_{sim} defined above to rerank for each sentence the n-best hypotheses of an MT system. The coreference similarity is not measured individually for each sentence, but at the document level. Our goal is to find a combination of translations that optimizes this global score.

For this purpose, we use the Moses toolkit to build a phrase-based statistical MT system (Koehn et al., 2007), with training data from the translation task of the WMT 2013 workshop (Bojar et al., 2013). The English-Spanish training set consists of 14 million sentences, with approximately 340 million tokens. The tuning set is the *News Test 2010-2011* one, with ca. 5,500 sentences and almost 120k tokens. We built a 4-gram language model from the same training data augmented by ca. 5,500 sentences monolingual data from *News Test 2015*. Our baseline system has a BLEU score of 30.8 on the *News Test 2013* with 3,000 sentences.

We thus model the problem as follows. A translated document d_t is represented as an array of translations $d_t = (s^1, s^2, ..., s^M)$, where each sentence can be selected from a list of n-best translation hypotheses $s^i \in \{s^i_1, s^i_2, ..., s^i_N\}$. The objective is to select the best combination of hypotheses based on their coreference similarity C_{sim} with the source, i.e.:

$$\arg\max_{h_1, h_2, .., h_M} C_{sim}((s^1_{h_1}, s^2_{h_2}, ..., s^m_{h_M}), d_s)$$

To limit the decrease of sentence-level translation scores when optimizing the document-level objective, we keep track of the former and select the sentences with the best translation scores if they lead to the same C_{sim}.

This combinatorial problem is expensive, so we try to reduce the search space to allow reasonable performance. First, we filter out candidate sentences. In this approach, the important variations in translation are the mentions, thus sentences are modeled as sets of mentions and duplicate sets are filtered out. Second, we apply beam search optimization. Based on the fact that the first mentions of entities usually contain more information than the next ones, the beam search starts from the first sentence and aggregates at each step the translation hypothesis with the highest similarity scores with the preceding ones.

We foresee several limitations of this approach. First, with a sentence containing several mentions, there is no guarantee that the n-best hypotheses include a combination of mention translations that optimize all mentions as the same time. What is worse, the correct translation of a given mention may not be present at all among the n-best hypotheses, because the differences among the top hypotheses are often very small, especially when sentences are long. In order to solve these problems, we present a second approach.

5 Post-editing Mentions Based on Mention Pair and MT Scores

This approach differs from the previous one in two aspects. First, it uses hypotheses of translation of individual coreferent mentions rather than of complete sentences. This allows to optimize the translation of each mention independently, and to increase the variety of hypotheses of each mention. Second, coreference resolution is applied only in the source side. So, instead of searching for similar clustering in the target side, we try to induce it. The selection of the best translation hypothesis of a mention is based on a cluster-level coreference score. We choose the hypothesis that correlates better with other mentions in the same cluster. This method improves the performance because it uses coreference resolution only once instead of multiple times, and as shown in the experimental section, it is more effective at improving the translation of mentions.

5.1 Selecting Candidate Translations

In order to obtain the n-best translation hypotheses of the mentions, it is important to include the surrounding context in the translation, otherwise, an independent translation could lead to the construction of invalid or erroneous sentences.

We would like to have a MT system that brings hypotheses corresponding only to mentions and fix the translations of other word, in a way that we can interchange the hypotheses of one mention in the same text. Building such MT system would require a significant modification of the baseline.

As an alternative solution, we will simply perform two passes of MT. The first pass is a simple translation of the text. Then, the mentions are identified in the target text and they are replaced by their source-language version. This results into a mixed language text that will be passed a second time to the MT system, so that the system will identify and translate only the words in the source language. Nevertheless, the language and reordering models are still going to evaluate on the complete sentence. To avoid any translation of the context words (i.e. not mentions) in the second pass, we filter out from the translation table all words not corresponding to mentions.

It is important to note that we consider only the heads of mentions obtained from the parse tree (this annotation is included in AnCora corpus), in order to avoid long mentions such as the ones with subordinate clauses, and focus on the most important part of each mention.

5.2 Cluster-level Coreference Score

In this approach, we rely on the coreference resolver applied to the source side to define the clusters of mentions. Each cluster is defined as a set of mentions $c_x = \{m^i, m^j, .., m^k\}$, where each mention can be selected from a set of translation hypotheses $m^i \in \{m^i_1, m^i_2, ..., m^i_N\}$.

By definition, the mentions in a cluster represent the same entity. Thus, they have to correlate in features such as gender, number, animation, etc. In order to achieve this objective in the target side, we define a cluster-level coreference score C_{ss}. It represents the likelihood that all mentions in that cluster belong to the same entity. So, for each given cluster, we select the combination of translation hypotheses of mentions with higher cluster-level coreference score.

This combinatorial problem is expensive, therefore, it is simplified with a beam search approach. Mentions are processed one at a time. The translation hypotheses of a new upcoming mention are compared with each of the previously selected ones. Then, the combinations with lower C_{ss} are pruned. The algorithm continue in the same manner until it processes the last mention.

In order to compare two mentions, we use the mention pair scorer from (Clark and Manning, 2015). It uses a logistic classifier to assign a probability to a pair of hypotheses, which represents the likelihood that they are coreferent. The pair score is defined as follows:

$$p_{pair}(m^i_{h_i}, m^j_{h_j}) = (1 + e^{\theta^T f(m^i_{h_i}, m^j_{h_j})})^{-1}$$

where $f(m^i_{h_i}, m^j_{h_j})$ is a vector of feature functions of the mentions and θ is the vector of feature weights. Finally, we define the cluster-level coreference score C_{ss} as the product of the individual pairwise probabilities:

$$C_{ss}(c_x) = \prod_{m^i \in c_x} \prod_{m^{i \neq j} \in c_x} p_{pair}(m^i_{h_i}, m^j_{h_j})$$

We illustrate this idea with an example. Here, we have a sentence in Spanish and its translation to English. We show one coreference cluster c_1 formed by three mentions:

Source (es): *La alcaldesa de Málaga y cabeza del* $[partido]_{c_1}$ $[que]_{c_1}$ *ganó en esta ciudad, pidió a los militantes de* $[este\ partido\ político]_{c_1}$*...*

Target (en): *The mayor of Malaga and head of the* $[m_1]_{c_1}$ $[m_2]_{c_1}$ *won in this city, asked the militants of this* $[m_3]_{c_1}$ *to...*

In this example, the three marked mentions have the following translation hypotheses: $m_1 \in \{match, party\}$, $m_2 \in \{who, which\}$, and $m_3 \in \{political\ party\}$. We calculate the pairwise score p_{pair} of each combination and show the results in the following table.

m_1, m_2	$(match, who) = 0.03$, $(match, which) =$ **0.35**, $(party, who) = 0.01$, $(party, which) =$ **0.26**
m_1, m_3	$(match, political\ party) = 0.08$, $(party, political\ party) =$ **0.53**
m_2, m_3	$(political\ party, who) = 0.12$, $(political\ party, which) =$ **0.27**

Finally, we find that the set of translation hypotheses with the highest cluster-level coreference C_{ss} score is {'party', 'which', 'political party'}, with a score of 0.04. Intuitively, we can verify that this final combination is the best solution for the example.

5.3 Incorporating Entity and Translation Information

The proposed score guides the system to select translation hypotheses which are more likely to refer to the same entity in a cluster. In order to enhance the decision process, we include two sources of additional information: the translation frequency, that can help to decide between synonyms by selecting the most frequently translated one; and information of the entity in the source side, which enriches the knowledge of the entity.

The information about frequency of translation can indicate how well a particular hypothesis translates the mention. Therefore, we define a translation score, T_s, at mention-level. The translation score of a hypothesis is calculated based on its relative frequency of emission by the MT system, as follows:

$$T_s(m^i_{hi}) = count(m^i_{hi}) / \sum_j count(m^i_j)$$

The information about the entity in source side can indicate how well a particular hypothesis represents it. Thus, we define a simple representation of an entity by setting relevant features such as gender, number, and animation. The features are extracted and summarized from all mentions in the cluster. This is a naive representation, and more advanced work on entity-level representations has been performed in relation to coreference resolution (Clark and Manning, 2016; Wiseman et al., 2016), which could be applied here in the future.

Having an entity representation, we define a simple scoring function which measures how well a candidate represents an entity with respect to other alternatives:

$$E_s(m_{hi}^i = f(m_{h_i}^i, \theta_{e_x}) / \sum_j f(m_j^i, \theta_{e_x})$$

where f is a linear function and θ_{e_x} are the entity features.

5.4 Combining Scores

Finally, the decision is made through the combination of the three previous scores: cluster-level coreference, translation, and entity matching. As one additional step, we adjust the coreference score to the same scale as others:

$$C_s = C_{ss}(m_{h_i}^i, m_{h_j}^j, \ldots) / \sum_{x,y,\ldots} C_{ss}(m_x^i, m_y^j, \ldots).$$

The final score is defined as follows:

$$\begin{aligned} C_{score}(m_{h_i}^i, m_{h_j}^j, \ldots) =& C_s(m_{h_i}^i, m_{h_j}^j, \ldots)^{\lambda_1} \times \\ & [T_s(m_{h_i}^i).T_s(m_{h_j}^j) \ldots]^{\lambda_2} \times \\ & [E_s(m_{h_i}^i).E_s(m_{h_j}^j) \ldots]^{\lambda_3} \end{aligned}$$

where $\sum_i \lambda_i = 1$ are predefined hyper-parameters of the function. The final set is given by:

$$(m^i, m^j, \ldots) = \underset{h_i, h_j, \ldots}{\arg\max} \quad C_{score}(m_{h_i}^i, m_{h_j}^j, \ldots).$$

These three hyper-parameters were optimized on a different subset of AnCora-ES than the one used for evaluation. The optimized values are λ_1=0.5, λ_2=0.1, and λ_3=0.4.

6 Experimental Results

The objective of our initial experiments is to measure how much coreference can improve the correct choices of translation of mentions, and impact of these choices on global translation quality. We translated 10 sample documents from the test set to serve as reference translations for evaluation.

6.1 Evaluation with Automatic Metrics

The evaluation of global MT quality is made with the well-known BLEU n-gram precision metric (Papineni et al., 2002), while the evaluation of mentions, being less standardized, is performed in several ways. We reuse previous insights on pronoun translation and therefore score them with a metric that automatically computes the accuracy of pronoun translation (APT) in terms of number of pronouns that are identical vs. different from a human reference translation (Miculicich Werlen and Popescu-Belis, 2016)[5].

More originally, in order to provide a complete view of the performance, we compute the "accuracy of noun translation" (ANT), by reusing the same idea as in APT to count the number of exactly matched nouns between MT and the reference translation.

We test the two proposed methods re-ranking and post-editing vs. the phrase-based statistical MT (PBSMT) baseline described in Section 4.3. We also include a neural machine translation (NMT) baseline (Bahdanau et al., 2015) as a reference for comparison. We chose to build our systems over a PBSMT system for simplicity, because the word-alignment can be obtained directly from the system. Additionally, we also present the results obtained with an automatic coreference resolver in the source side, namely the CorZu system (Tuggener, 2016; Rios, 2015), for the post-editing approach.

Table 3 shows the results of the experiments. We first calculate BLEU, APT, and ANT values at document-level, and show the values of the average and standard deviation for the three evaluated systems: baseline, and our two proposed approaches. Additionally, we show the significance levels (t-test) of the results in comparison to the

System	Metric BLEU	APT	ANT
Baseline PBSMT	46.5±4.3	0.35±0.07	0.78±0.08
Baseline NMT	46.9±3.7	0.37±0.07	0.78±0.07
PBSMT + Re-rank	41.7±3.9***	0.40±0.10*	0.74±0.01**
PBSMT + Post-edit	46.4±3.9	0.59±0.13***	0.78±0.07
PBSMT + Post-edit + Automatic coreference	46.1±4.3	0.41±0.07*	0.76±0.09

Table 3: Comparison of baseline MT and our proposals for reranking or post-editing, for three metrics. In addition to the average scores and standard deviation over the ten test documents, we indicate the statistical significance level of the difference between each of our systems and the baseline (* for 95.0%, ** for 99.0% and *** for 99.9%).

[5] https://github.com/idiap/APT

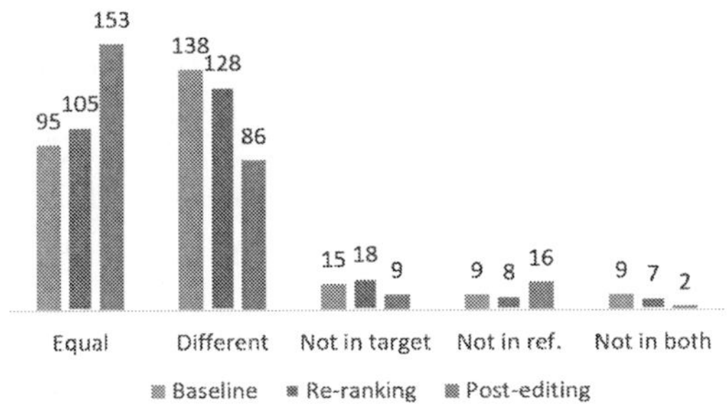

Figure 1: Pronoun translation in comparison with the reference: numbers of equal vs. different pronouns for the three systems, including also missing pronouns in target, reference, and both sides (counts based on source pronouns).

baseline. The post-editing approach improves the pronoun translation quite significantly, without decreasing the overall quality of translation. This improvement is demonstrated by the rise of APT score, whereas BLUE score remains without significant change. However, the quality of the translation of nouns does not change significantly, as shown by the ANT.

The re-ranking approach shows a significant increase in the quality of pronoun translation. Nevertheless, the overall quality of translation decreases significantly, as well as the quality of noun translation. These results can be explained by the limitations of this approach. The optimization was done by taking into account the correlation of mentions, but the changes were made at sentence level, and the overall quality of translation at sentence level was not considered. To address this problem, a combination of coreference similarity and translation probability for each sentence could be used in future.

Figure 1 shows the distribution of pronouns translated by the three evaluated systems (i.e. baseline, re-ranking, and post-editing) in comparison with the reference. The number of pronouns equal to the reference increases for both proposed approaches, specially for the post-editing. The pronouns that improve the most were the third-person personal and possessive ones. Also, the translation of some of the null pronouns in the source was improved. The association with other mentions of the same entity, and the representation of the entity coming from the source side was important for this improvement.

Evaluation	System Baseline	Re-rank	Post-edit
No. '0' (wrong)	53	55	21
No. '1' (acceptable)	21	19	28
No. '2' (eq. to ref.)	115	115	140
Sum of the scores	251	249	308

Table 4: Manual evaluation of fourth randomly selected documents. The evaluation was done over nouns and pronouns.

6.2 Human Evaluation

Finally, we perform manual evaluation by examining source mentions, as annotated over AnCora-ES, and evaluating their individual translations by the baseline MT along with the two approaches presented above (in Sections 4 vs. 5). When presented to the evaluator, the three translations of each source sentence are provided in a random order, so that the evaluator does not know to which system they belong. The evaluator assigned a score of '2' to a translation identical to the reference, '1' for translation that is different but still good or acceptable, and '0' to a wrong or unacceptable translation. To minimize the time spent on manual evaluation at this stage, one evaluator rated four test documents.

Table 4 shows the results of the manual evaluation, scored as explained above, which includes nouns and pronouns together. In general, it supports the results of the automatic evaluation. Here, the post-editing approach has 32 less mentions scored as "wrong" than the baseline, 7 of them were score as "acceptable", and the rest 25 as identical to the reference. The re-ranking approach, despite the theoretical appeal of its definition, fails to improve noun and pronoun translation.

Table 5 shows examples of translations obtained with our approaches. The translations of nouns are already good for the baseline, and the differences are in many cases due to the use of synonyms and acronyms. Still, there are source nouns that suffer from sense ambiguity, which may be improved by our method. However, this particular test set is too small and does not contain enough instances of this type to evaluate their translations with certainty.

7 Conclusion

We have presented two methods for improving noun and pronoun translation based on coreference similarity of source and translated texts.

Correctly modified examples
S: *[Barton]$_3$, por [su]$_3$ parte , también dudó de la capacidad de [Megawati]$_2$ en [su]$_3$ [nueva tarea]$_4$.* **R:** *[Barton]$_3$, for [his]$_3$ part , also doubted [Megawati]$_2$'s ability in [her]$_2$ [new task]$_4$.* **B:** *[Barton]$_3$, for [its]$_3$ part , also doubted the capacity of Megawati in [his]$_2$ [new task]$_4$.* **P:** *[Barton]$_3$, for [his]$_3$ part , also doubted the capacity of [Megawati]$_2$ in [her]$_2$ [new task]$_4$.* **S:** *... que " [parece estar]$_2$ abrumada ... críticos consideran que [no será]$_2$ capaz de hacerse con el papel de líder .* **R:** *...that " [she seems]$_2$ overwhelmed ... critics consider [she will not be]$_2$ able to take the lead role .* **B:** *... that " [appears to be]$_2$ overwhelmed ... critics believe that [it will not be]$_2$ able to take a leading role .* **P:** *...that " [she seems]$_2$ to be overwhelmed ... critics believe that [she will not be]$_2$ able to take a leading role .*
Incorrectly modified example
S: *- [Es]$_1$ iconoclasta por valenciano ? - .* **R:**: *- [Are you]$_1$ iconoclastic by Valencian ? - .* **B:** *- [Is]$_1$ an iconoclast by Valencian ? - .* **P:** *- [he is]$_1$ an iconoclast by Valencian ? - .*

Table 5: Examples of source, reference, baseline and post-edited sentences.

While the re-ranking approach did not achieve its goals, the post-editing approach brought a significant improvement of Spanish-to-English pronoun translation. This should be confirmed, in the future, by more detailed measurements on larger data sets. Also, one simplifying assumption, namely the use of ground-truth coreference annotation on the target side (here, from AnCora-ES) should be relaxed, in order to address the challenge of using automated coreference resolution on both source and target sides – and thus produce a fully-automated, unrestricted MT system.

This study contributes to a growing body of research on modeling longer range dependencies than those modeled in phrase-based or neural MT, across different sentences of a document. The Docent decoder (Hardmeier et al., 2012), which uses document-level features to improve coherence across translated sentences, could also be used in combination with the coreference similarity score, or, alternatively, neural MT could be adapted to take advantage of neural network representations of coreference information.

Acknowledgments

We are grateful for support to the Swiss National Science Foundation (SNSF) under the Sinergia MODERN project (grant n. 147653, see `www.idiap.ch/project/modern/`) and to the European Union under the Horizon 2020 SUMMA project (grant n. 688139, see `www.summa-project.eu`). We thank the CORBON anonymous reviewers for their helpful suggestions.

References

Amit Bagga and Breck Baldwin. 1998. Algorithms for scoring coreference chains. In *Proceedings of the First International Conference on Language Resources and Evaluation Workshop on Linguistics Coreference*, volume 1, pages 563–566, Granada, Spain.

Dzmitry Bahdanau, Kyunghyun Cho, and Yoshua Bengio. 2015. Neural machine translation by jointly learning to align and translate. In *Proceedings of the International Conference on Learning Representations (ICLR)*, San Diego, USA.

Eric Bengtson and Dan Roth. 2008. Understanding the value of features for coreference resolution. In *Proceedings of the 2008 Conference on Empirical Methods in Natural Language Processing*, pages 294–303, Honolulu, Hawaii, October. Association for Computational Linguistics.

Ondřej Bojar, Christian Buck, Chris Callison-Burch, Christian Federmann, Barry Haddow, Philipp Koehn, Christof Monz, Matt Post, Radu Soricut, and Lucia Specia. 2013. Findings of the 2013 Workshop on statistical machine translation. In *Proceedings of the Eighth Workshop on Statistical Machine Translation*, pages 1–44, Sofia, Bulgaria, August. Association for Computational Linguistics.

Jimmy Callin, Christian Hardmeier, and Jörg Tiedemann. 2015. Part-of-speech driven cross-lingual pronoun prediction with feed-forward neural networks. In *Proceedings of the Second Workshop on Discourse in Machine Translation*, pages 59–64, Lisbon, Portugal, September. Association for Computational Linguistics.

Kevin Clark and Christopher D. Manning. 2015. Entity-centric coreference resolution with model stacking. In *Proceedings of the 53rd Annual Meeting of the Association for Computational Linguistics and the 7th International Joint Conference on Natural Language Processing (Volume 1: Long Papers)*, pages 1405–1415, Beijing, China, July. Association for Computational Linguistics.

Kevin Clark and Christopher D. Manning. 2016. Improving coreference resolution by learning entity-level distributed representations. In *Proceedings of the 54th Annual Meeting of the Association for Computational Linguistics (Volume 1: Long Papers)*, pages 643–653, Berlin, Germany, August. Association for Computational Linguistics.

Raj Dabre, Yevgeniy Puzikov, Fabien Cromieres, and Sadao Kurohashi. 2016. The Kyoto University cross-lingual pronoun translation system. In *Proceedings of the First Conference on Machine Translation*, pages 571–575, Berlin, Germany, August. Association for Computational Linguistics.

Eraldo Fernandes, Cícero dos Santos, and Ruy Milidiú. 2012. Latent structure perceptron with feature induction for unrestricted coreference resolution. In *Joint Conference on EMNLP and CoNLL - Shared Task*, pages 41–48, Jeju Island, Korea, July. Association for Computational Linguistics.

Liane Guillou, Christian Hardmeier, Preslav Nakov, Sara Stymne, Jörg Tiedemann, Yannick Versley, Mauro Cettolo, Bonnie Webber, and Andrei Popescu-Belis. 2016. Findings of the 2016 WMT shared task on cross-lingual pronoun prediction. In *Proceedings of the First Conference on Machine Translation*, pages 525–542, Berlin, Germany, August. Association for Computational Linguistics.

Liane Guillou. 2012. Improving pronoun translation for statistical machine translation. In *Proceedings of the Student Research Workshop at the 13th Conference of the European Chapter of the Association for Computational Linguistics*, pages 1–10, Avignon, France, April. Association for Computational Linguistics.

Christian Hardmeier and Marcello Federico. 2010. Modelling pronominal anaphora in statistical machine translation. In *IWSLT (International Workshop on Spoken Language Translation)*, pages 283–289, Paris, France, December.

Christian Hardmeier, Joakim Nivre, and Jörg Tiedemann. 2012. Document-wide decoding for phrase-based statistical machine translation. In *Proceedings of the 2012 Joint Conference on Empirical Methods in Natural Language Processing and Computational Natural Language Learning*, pages 1179–1190, Jeju Island, Korea, July. Association for Computational Linguistics.

Christian Hardmeier, Preslav Nakov, Sara Stymne, Jörg Tiedemann, Yannick Versley, and Mauro Cettolo. 2015. Pronoun-focused MT and cross-lingual pronoun prediction: Findings of the 2015 DiscoMT shared task on pronoun translation. In *Proceedings of the Second Workshop on Discourse in Machine Translation*, pages 1–16, Lisbon, Portugal, September. Association for Computational Linguistics.

Philipp Koehn, Hieu Hoang, Alexandra Birch, Chris Callison-Burch, Marcello Federico, Nicola Bertoldi, Brooke Cowan, Wade Shen, Christine Moran, Richard Zens, Chris Dyer, Ondrej Bojar, Alexandra Constantin, and Evan Herbst. 2007. Moses: Open source toolkit for statistical machine translation. In *Proceedings of the 45th Annual Meeting of the Association for Computational Linguistics Companion Volume Proceedings of the Demo and Poster Sessions*, pages 177–180, Prague, Czech Republic, June. Association for Computational Linguistics.

Ronan Le Nagard and Philipp Koehn. 2010. Aiding pronoun translation with co-reference resolution. In *Proceedings of the Joint Fifth Workshop on Statistical Machine Translation and MetricsMATR*, pages 252–261, Uppsala, Sweden, July. Association for Computational Linguistics.

Heeyoung Lee, Yves Peirsman, Angel Chang, Nathanael Chambers, Mihai Surdeanu, and Dan Jurafsky. 2011. Stanford's multi-pass sieve coreference resolution system at the CoNLL-2011 shared task. In *Proceedings of the Fifteenth Conference on Computational Natural Language Learning: Shared Task*, pages 28–34, Portland, Oregon, USA, June. Association for Computational Linguistics.

Xiaoqiang Luo. 2005. On coreference resolution performance metrics. In *Proceedings of the Conference on Human Language Technology and Empirical Methods in Natural Language Processing*, pages 25–32, Vancouver, B.C., Canada.

Ngoc Quang Luong and Andrei Popescu-Belis. 2016. Improving pronoun translation by modeling coreference uncertainty. In *Proceedings of the First Conference on Machine Translation*, pages 12–20, Berlin, Germany, August. Association for Computational Linguistics.

Ngoc Quang Luong and Andrei Popescu-Belis. 2017. Machine translation of Spanish personal and possessive pronouns using anaphora probabilities. In *Proceedings of the 15th Conference of the European Chapter of the Association for Computational Linguistics (EACL)*, Valencia, Spain, April.

Ngoc Quang Luong, Lesly Miculicich Werlen, and Andrei Popescu-Belis. 2015. Pronoun translation and prediction with or without coreference links. In *Proceedings of the Second Workshop on Discourse in Machine Translation*, pages 94–100, Lisbon, Portugal, September. Association for Computational Linguistics.

Juhani Luotolahti, Jenna Kanerva, and Filip Ginter. 2016. Cross-lingual pronoun prediction with deep recurrent neural networks. In *Proceedings of the First Conference on Machine Translation*, pages 596–601, Berlin, Germany, August. Association for Computational Linguistics.

Christopher Manning, Mihai Surdeanu, John Bauer, Jenny Finkel, Steven Bethard, and David McClosky. 2014. The Stanford CoreNLP natural language processing toolkit. In *Proceedings of 52nd Annual Meeting of the Association for Computational Linguistics: System Demonstrations*, pages 55–60, Baltimore, Maryland, June. Association for Computational Linguistics.

Lluís Màrquez, Marta Recasens, and Emili Sapena. 2013. Coreference resolution: an empirical study based on SemEval-2010 Shared Task 1. *Language Resources and Evaluation*, 47(3):661–694.

Lesly Miculicich Werlen and Andrei Popescu-Belis. 2016. Validation of an automatic metric for the accuracy of pronoun translation (APT). Technical Report Idiap-RR-29-2016, Idiap Research Institute.

Ruslan Mitkov. 2002. *Anaphora Resolution*. Longman, London, UK.

Vincent Ng. 2010. Supervised noun phrase coreference research: The first fifteen years. In *Proceedings of the 48th Annual Meeting of the Association for Computational Linguistics*, pages 1396–1411, Uppsala, Sweden, July. Association for Computational Linguistics.

Kishore Papineni, Salim Roukos, Todd Ward, and Wei-Jing Zhu. 2002. BLEU: a method for automatic evaluation of machine translation. In *Proceedings of 40th Annual Meeting of the Association for Computational Linguistics*, pages 311–318, Philadelphia, Pennsylvania, USA, July. Association for Computational Linguistics.

Andrei Popescu-Belis. 1999. Evaluation numérique de la résolution de la référence: Critiques et propositions. *TAL: Traitement automatique des langues*, 40(2):117–146.

Sameer Pradhan, Xiaoqiang Luo, Marta Recasens, Eduard Hovy, Vincent Ng, and Michael Strube. 2014. Scoring coreference partitions of predicted mentions: A reference implementation. In *Proceedings of the 52nd Annual Meeting of the Association for Computational Linguistics (Volume 2: Short Papers)*, pages 30–35, Baltimore, Maryland, June. Association for Computational Linguistics.

Marta Recasens and Eduard Hovy. 2011. BLANC: Implementing the Rand index for coreference evaluation. *Natural Language Engineering*, 17(4):485–510.

Marta Recasens and M. Antònia Martí. 2010. Ancora-CO: Coreferentially annotated corpora for Spanish and Catalan. *Language Resources and Evaluation*, 44(4):315–345.

Marta Recasens, Lluís Màrquez, Emili Sapena, M. Antònia Martí, Mariona Taulé, Véronique Hoste, Massimo Poesio, and Yannick Versley. 2010. SemEval-2010 task 1: Coreference resolution in multiple languages. In *Proceedings of the 5th International Workshop on Semantic Evaluation*, pages 1–8, Uppsala, Sweden, July. Association for Computational Linguistics.

Annette Rios. 2015. *A Basic Language Technology Toolkit for Quechua*. Ph.D. thesis, University of Zurich, January.

Don Tuggener. 2016. *Incremental Coreference Resolution for German*. Ph.D. thesis, University of Zurich.

Marc Vilain, John Burger, John Aberdeen, Dennis Connolly, and Lynette Hirschman. 1995. A model-theoretic coreference scoring scheme. In *Proceedings of the 6th Conference on Message Understanding*, pages 45–52, Columbia, MD, USA.

Sam Wiseman, Alexander M. Rush, Stuart Shieber, and Jason Weston. 2015. Learning anaphoricity and antecedent ranking features for coreference resolution. In *Proceedings of the 53rd Annual Meeting of the Association for Computational Linguistics and the 7th International Joint Conference on Natural Language Processing (Volume 1: Long Papers)*, pages 1416–1426, Beijing, China, July. Association for Computational Linguistics.

Sam Wiseman, Alexander M. Rush, and Stuart M. Shieber. 2016. Learning global features for coreference resolution. In *Proceedings of the 2016 Conference of the North American Chapter of the Association for Computational Linguistics: Human Language Technologies*, pages 994–1004, San Diego, California, June. Association for Computational Linguistics.

Multi-source annotation projection of coreference chains: assessing strategies and testing opportunities

Yulia Grishina and **Manfred Stede**
Applied Computational Linguistics
FSP Cognitive Science
University of Potsdam
grishina|stede@uni-potsdam.de

Abstract

In this paper, we examine the possibility of using annotation projection from multiple sources for automatically obtaining coreference annotations in the target language. We implement a multi-source annotation projection algorithm and apply it on an English-German-Russian parallel corpus in order to transfer coreference chains from two sources to the target side. Operating in two settings – a low-resource and a more linguistically-informed one – we show that automatic coreference transfer could benefit from combining information from multiple languages, and assess the quality of both the extraction and the linking of target coreference mentions.

1 Introduction

While monolingual coreference resolution systems are being constantly improved, multilingual coreference resolution has received much less attention in the NLP community. Most of the coreference systems can only work on English data and are not ready to be adapted to other languages. Developing a coreference resolution system for a new language from scratch is challenging due to its technical complexity and the variability of coreference phenomena in different languages, and it depends on high-quality language technologies (such as mention extraction, syntactic parsing, named entity recognition) as well as gold standard data, which are not available for a wide range of languages.

However, this can be alleviated by using cross-lingual projection which allows for transferring existing methods or resources across languages. There have been some influential work on annotation projection for different NLP tasks which performed quite well cross-lingually, e.g. for semantic role labelling (Akbik et al., 2015) or syntactic parsing (Lacroix et al., 2016). At the same time, several recent studies on annotation projection for coreference have proven it to be a more difficult task than POS tagging or syntactic parsing, which is hard to be tackled by projection algorithms. These works are limited to the existing multilingual resources (mostly newswire, mostly CoNLL 2012 (Pradhan et al., 2012)) and, surprisingly, are not even able to beat a threshold of 40.0 F1 for coreference resolvers trained on projections only. The best-performing system based on projection achieves 38.82 for English-Spanish and 37.23 for English-Portuguese F1-score (Martins, 2015), while state-of-the-art monolingual coreference systems are already able to achieve 64.21 F-score for English (Wiseman et al., 2016). While being quite powerful for other tasks, annotation projection is less successful for coreference resolution. Therefore, our question is, how can the quality of annotation projection be improved for the task of coreference resolution?

In our opinion, projection from multiple source languages can be a long-term solution, assuming that we have access to two or more reliable coreference resolvers on the source sides. Our idea is that multi-source annotation projection for coreference resolution would grant a bigger pool of potential mentions to choose from, which can be beneficial for overcoming language divergences. Therefore, the main goals of this study are: (a) to explore different strategies of multi-source projection of coreference chains on a small experimental corpus, and (b) to evaluate the projection errors and assess the prospects of this approach for multilingual coreference resolution.

This paper is structured as follows: The related work is discussed in Section 2, and the dataset is presented in Section 3. The methodology adapted

Proceedings of the 2nd Workshop on Coreference Resolution Beyond OntoNotes (CORBON 2017), co-located with EACL 2017, pages 41–50,
Valencia, Spain, April 4, 2017.

for our experiments is explained in Section 4. We then analyse the projection errors and evaluate the target annotations (Section 5). Finally, Section 6 summarises the outcomes of this study, and Section 7 concludes.

2 Related work

Annotation projection is a method of automatically transferring linguistic annotations from one language to the other in a parallel corpus. It was first applied in the pilot work of Yarowski et al. (2001) who used this technique to induce POS and Named Entity taggers, NP chunkers and morphological analyzers for different languages. In particular, they used labelled English data and an aligned parallel corpus to automatically create mappings between the annotations from the source side and the corresponding aligned words on the target side, and exploited the resulting annotations to train their systems.

Thereafter, projection has been widely used as a method in cross-lingual NLP, and several studies on annotation projection targeted cross-lingual coreference resolution. In particular, automatic annotation transfer was first applied to coreference chains by Postolache et al. (2006) who used a projection method and filtering heuristics to support the creation of a coreference corpus in a new language. The evaluation of projected annotations against a small manually annotated corpus exhibited promising 63.88 and 82.6 MUC and B-cubed scores respectively. Subsequently, Souza and Orăsan (2011) went one step further and made an attempt to project automatically produced annotations, and used projected data to train a new coreference resolver, which, however, resulted in a poor coreference resolution quality due to low-quality annotations on the source side.

The next steps in projecting coreference included several translation-based approaches. The difference is that the target text is first translated into the source language, on which coreference resolution is performed; after that, the source coreference chains can be projected back to the target side. This approach was used, for example, by Rahman and Ng (2012) to train coreference resolvers for Spanish and Italian using English as the source language, achieving an average F1 of 37.6 and 21.4 for Spanish and Italian respectively in a low-resource scenario, and much better scores of 46.8 and 54.9 F1 using only a mention extractor. Similarly, Ogrodniczuk (2013) experimented with translation-based projection for English and Polish using only a mention extractor. The evaluation of the quality of the projected annotations on manually annotated data showed 70.31 F1.

The most recent application of projection to coreference is due to Martins (2015) who experimented with transferring automatically produced coreference chains from English to Spanish and Portuguese, and subsequently trained target coreference resolvers on the projected data, combining projection with posterior regularization. His approach shows competitive results in a low-resource setting, with the average of 38.82 F1 for coreference resolution systems trained on projections for Spanish and 37.23 for Portuguese, as compared to the performance of fully supervised systems: 43.93 and 39.83 respectively.

The idea of using multiple sources for annotation projection was also initially considered by Yarowsky et al. (2001) who used multiple translations of the same text to improve the performance of the projected annotations for several NLP tasks. Furthermore, multi-source projection has been extensively explored for multilingual syntactic parsing. The best unsupervised dependency parsers nowadays rely on annotation projection (Rasooli and Collins, 2015; Johannsen et al., 2016). To our knowledge, there has been no attempt to apply multi-source annotation projection to the task of coreference resolution so far.

3 Data

For our experiments, we have chosen a trilingual parallel annotated coreference corpus of English, German and Russian from (Grishina and Stede, 2015). This corpus was annotated with coreference chains according to the guidelines described in (Grishina and Stede, 2016) which are largely compatible to the coreference annotations of the OntoNotes corpus (Pradhan and Xue, 2009). The corpus is annotated with full coreference chains, excluding singletons[1]. The major differences to OntoNotes are: (a) annotation of NPs only, but not of verbs that are coreferent with NPs, (b) inclusion of appositions into the markable span and not marking them as a separate relation, (c) marking relative pronouns as separate markables, and (d)

[1]Mentions of the entities that appear in the text only once.

	News			Stories			Total		
	EN	DE	RU	EN	DE	RU	EN	DE	RU
Sentences	229	229	229	184	184	184	413	413	413
Tokens	6033	6158	5785	2711	2595	2307	8744	8753	8092
Markables	560	586	604	466	491	471	1026	1077	1075
Chains	115	133	133	40	40	45	155	173	178

Table 1: Corpus statistics for English, German and Russian

annotation of pronominal adverbs[2] in German if they co-refer with an NP.

Since the corpus was already aligned bilingually for two language pairs – English-German and English-Russian – we first align the German-Russian corpus at the sentence level using LF Aligner[3] and then select parallel sentences present in all the three languages. This method reduces the average number of sentences per language by 5% and the average number of coreference chains per language by 6% (as compared to the corpus statistics published by Grishina and Stede (2015)). Then we re-run GIZA++ word aligner (Och and Ney, 2003) on the resulting sentences for all the language combinations with German and Russian as targets.

The statistics of the experiment corpus after selecting only trilingual sentences are presented in Table 1.

4 Experiments

Combining information coming from two or more languages is a more challenging task as compared to single-source projection where one just transfers all the information from one language to the other. For coreference, this task is non-trivial (as opposed to, for instance, multi-source projection of POS information where an intuitive majority voting strategy could be chosen), since we cannot operate on the token level and even not on the mention level: We cannot implement a strategy to choose e.g. the most frequent label for a token or a sequence of tokens (coreferent/non-coreferent), since they belong to mention clusters which are not aligned on the source sides. In other words, if mention x_a belongs to chain A in the first source language and mention y_b belongs to chain B in the second source language, and they are projected onto the same mention z_{ab} on the target side, we do not know whether both target chains A' and B' projected from A and B respectively and both containing the mention in question are equal or not, as we cannot rely on chain IDs which are not common across languages. Therefore, we have to operate on the chain level and first compare projected coreference chains. We treat coreference chains as clusters, measure the similarity between them and use this information to choose between them or combine them together in the projection.

Projecting coreference chains (=clusters of mentions) from more than one language, we can have the following cases:

(a) Two chains are identical (contain all the same mentions);

(b) Two chains are disjoint (contain no same mentions);

(c) Two chains overlap (contain some identical mentions).

While cases (a) and (b) are quite straightforward, case (c) is more difficult since we have to determine whether to treat these chains as being equal or not.

Following the work of (Rasooli and Collins, 2015), we rely upon two strategies – concatenation and voting – to process coreference chains coming from two sources. Since we only have two sources, instead of voting we implement intersection. In the case of coreference, we can enrich annotations from one language with the annotations from the other one or create a completely new set out of two projection sets. In particular, we experiment with several naive methods and evaluate their quality, and then combine them with each other in order to find the optimal strategy.

We implement the following methods:

(1) **Concatenation:** Data is obtained from each of the languages separately and then concatenated.

(a) `add`: Disjoint chains present in only one language are added to the projected

[2] Adverbs that are formed by combining a pronoun and a preposition, e.g. *therefor*.

[3] https://sourceforge.net/projects/aligner/

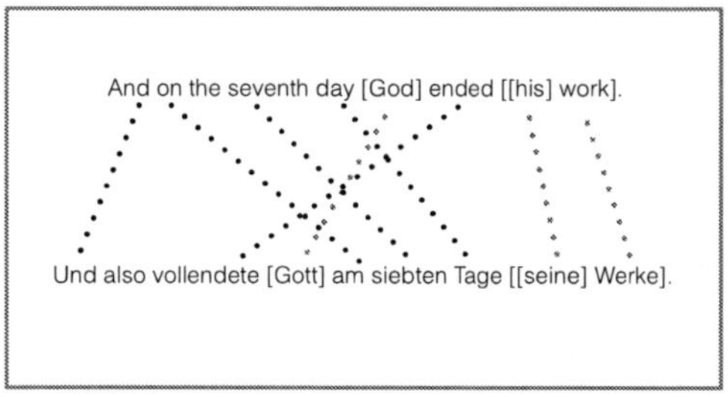

Figure 1: Direct projection algorithm

chains from the other language. Typically, we would take projected annotations for the best-scored language and enrich them with annotations from the less-scored language.

(b) `unify-concatenate (u-con):` Overlapping chains from both languages are merged together: If chain A and chain B overlap, we concatenate the mentions from both chains that form a new chain AB.

(2) **Intersection:** Projected annotations are obtained by intersecting projections coming from two sources.

(a) `intersect (int):` The intersection of coreference chains present in both languages is chosen[4].

(b) `unify-intersect (u-int):` The intersection of the mentions for overlapping chains is chosen: If chain A and chain B overlap, we intersect the mentions from both chains that form a new chain AB.

We use the following formula to estimate the overlap between two coreference chains:

$$\frac{2|A \cap B|}{|A| + |B|}, \quad (1)$$

where A and B are the number of mentions for coreference chains in question. We experiment with different values of overlap and choose the best one for each of the methods[5]. For `u-int`, we perform intersection of mentions for all the chains with mention overlap over 0.05. For `u-con`, we select chains with 0.5 overlap value for German and 0.7 for Russian. If the overlap is less than these values, we treat these chains as disjoint.

Each of the methods is applied in the following settings:

1. Setting 1: no additional linguistic information available. In this setting, we use only word alignments to transfer information from one language to the other.

2. Setting 2: a mention extractor is available. Relying on the output of the MATE dependency parser[6] (Bohnet, 2010) for German and the MALT dependency parser[7] (Nivre et al.,) for Russian[8], we automatically extract all mentions that have nouns, pronouns or pronominal adverbs as their heads. Thereafter, we map the output of the projection algorithm to the extracted mentions. We modify the mapping strategy described in (Rahman and Ng, 2012), mapping (a) projected markables that are identical to the extracted mentions, (b) projected markables that share the same right boundary with the extracted mentions, (c) markables that are spanned by the extracted mentions, (d) all other markables for which no corresponding mentions were found. Once a markable is mapped to a mention, we discard this mention, to ensure that it is not mapped to any other markable. For Russian, we skip step (b), which leads to better scores.

As the baseline, we select a single-source projection method. We re-implement a simple direct projection algorithm as described in (Postolache et al., 2006) and (Grishina and Stede, 2015), and we run it for the English-German, English-Russian, German-Russian and Russian-German language pairs, since we are not interested in projecting into English. The direct projection is illustrated in Fig.1 where coreference mentions *God*, *his* and *his work* are transferred to the German side via word alignments. Then, we run the algorithm in the two settings described above. Note that the projection results for setting 1 are slightly lower as compared to the results reported in (Grishina and Stede, 2015): we did not rely on intersective word

[4]Imagining we have more than two source languages, we could implement a more sophisticated voting scheme

[5]We use part of the corpus to determine optimal thresholds and the other one to obtain the results.

[6]https://code.google.com/archive/p/mate-tools/

[7]http://www.maltparser.org

[8]Using the model provided by Sharoff and Nivre (2011)

	MUC			B^3			$CEAF_m$			Avg.		
	P	R	F1	P	R	F1	P	R	F1	P	R	F1
EN→DE	57.6	46.0	51.1	47.3	35.6	40.4	61.1	49.7	54.7	55.3	43.8	48.7
RU→DE	43.3	28.4	34.1	33.3	18.9	23.5	46.2	32.7	38.1	40.9	26.7	31.9
EN,RU→DE:												
- `add`	52.7	46.1	49.1	41.5	36.5	38.6	53.5	51.2	52.2	49.2	44.6	46.6
- `int`	46.7	2.5	4.5	82.3	3.1	5.6	87.5	3.6	6.5	**72.2**	3.1	5.5
- `u-con`	56.0	48.8	52.1	44.5	38.8	41.3	59.4	51.9	55.3	53.3	**46.5**	**49.6**
- `u-int`	64.7	26.1	36.7	58.6	18.7	27.3	65.7	32.4	43.1	63.0	25.7	35.7
EN→DE+*ment*	66.7	53.1	59.0	54.8	41.6	47.0	68.1	55.3	61.1	63.2	50.0	55.7
RU→DE+*ment*:	43.6	28.5	34.2	34.3	19.1	24.0	47.1	33.4	38.8	41.7	27.0	32.3
EN,RU→DE												
- `add`+*ment*	60.0	53.1	56.2	47.0	42.7	44.3	57.9	56.9	57.2	55.0	50.9	52.6
- `int`+*ment*	56.7	3.6	6.3	96.7	4.5	7.9	97.8	4.9	8.6	**83.7**	4.3	7.6
- `u-con`+*ment*	66.1	55.7	60.4	53.4	45.0	48.6	67.4	57.4	61.9	62.3	**52.7**	**57.0**
- `u-int`+*ment*	73.7	29.6	41.7	68.1	21.6	31.3	73.6	36.1	48.0	71.8	29.1	40.3

Table 2: Results for German

	MUC			B^3			$CEAF_m$			Avg.		
	P	R	F1	P	R	F1	P	R	F1	P	R	F1
EN→RU	71.3	55.1	62.0	61.2	43.0	50.3	71.5	56.6	63.1	68.0	51.6	58.5
DE →RU:	59.1	32.0	41.3	46.8	19.6	27.3	57.3	35.1	43.3	54.4	28.9	37.3
EN,DE→RU												
- `add`	67.8	55.5	60.9	55.8	43.7	48.8	64.8	57.9	61.0	62.8	**52.4**	56.9
- `int`	87.5	3.0	5.9	85.0	4.3	8.2	85.0	4.8	9.0	**85.8**	4.0	7.7
- `u-con`	70.6	55.7	62.2	60.1	43.6	50.4	71.0	57.1	63.2	67.2	52.2	**58.6**
- `u-int`	81.6	29.3	42.9	74.8	19.5	30.6	77.6	35.5	48.6	78.0	28.1	40.7
EN→RU+*ment*	71.6	55.4	62.3	61.7	43.2	50.6	72.0	57.1	63.5	68.4	52.4	58.8
DE →RU+*ment*	59.2	32.0	41.4	47.5	19.7	27.6	57.9	35.4	43.8	54.9	29.0	37.6
EN,DE→RU												
- `add`+*ment*	68.0	55.7	61.1	56.7	44.1	49.3	65.1	58.3	61.4	63.3	**52.7**	57.3
- `int`+*ment*	87.5	2.4	4.7	85.0	3.5	6.6	85.0	3.9	7.5	**85.8**	3.3	6.3
- `u-con`+*ment*	70.9	56.0	62.4	60.9	43.9	50.8	71.5	57.5	63.6	67.7	52.5	**59.0**
- `u-int`+*ment*	82.2	29.2	42.9	76.4	19.4	30.6	78.7	35.7	49.0	79.1	28.1	40.8

Table 3: Results for Russian

alignments, since we were not interested in maximizing Precision at the cost of low Recall. Our goal was to obtain balanced scores to base our experiments upon.

The results for the baselines and the experiments are presented in Table 2 and Table 3. We compute the standard coreference metrics using the latest version of the CoNLL-2012 official scorer[9]. We also compute the average scores for all the coreference metrics.

5 Error analysis

We perform the error analysis by evaluating the projection quality for each of the methods described above. We first look at the common and distinct chains projected from two languages, and thereafter we evaluate the projection quality for different NP types and for the mentions of different length.

Common chains projected from two sources (`int`).

To analyse the common chains projected from two sources into German and Russian, we extract these chains from the target annotations and discard the singletons (if any). We compute the average chain length – 2.75 and 2.13 for German and Russian respectively – and look at the types of mentions that occur in these chains. Interestingly, string match is the most frequent type, e.g. 'Indien' - 'Indien', 'Афганистане' - 'которого' - 'Афганистане' ('Afghanistan' - 'which' - 'Afghanistan'). Named Entities form 46% of all the markables, followed by pronouns, which are 27% of all markables. Still, the Recall numbers are too low (3.1 and 4.0 for German and Russian) to apply this method on a small corpus.

[9] https://github.com/conll/reference-coreference-scorers

Distinct chains added from one source to the other (`add`). We examine the chains added from the less-scored language to the best-scored one by extracting these chains separately and computing their Precision. The results for both languages exhibit low Precision: 20.0 Precision for mention extraction and 15.0 average Precision for coreference, and 14.0 and 7.0 for German and Russian respectively. These numbers are too low to improve the projection performance in a low-resource setting.

Evaluation by NP type (`u-int, u-con`). In order to evaluate the projection quality for different NP types, we computed the distribution of types for the source and target annotations. For that reason, we POS-tagged the corpus using TreeTagger[10] (Schmid, 1995) with the pre-trained models for German and Russian. Subsequently, we extract the gold and the projected markables and compare them according to their types.

For German, we distinguish between the most frequent markable types: common NPs, Named Entities, personal, possessive, demonstrative and relative pronouns. For Russian, we only distinguish between the common NPs, Named Entities and pronouns, relying on the tagset available for TreeTagger[11]. Table 4 shows the distribution of all markables, regardless of whether they are correct or incorrect, for both the `u-int, u-con` settings. We do not show the percentage for the markables that are not of the types described below, but count them in the total numbers.

Interestingly, the percentage of NPs + Named Entites (computed together) and pronouns for both projections and for both methods is quite comparable (59.0 vs. 59.3, 54.7 vs. 58.4). However, the percentage of common NPs and Named Entities in German and Russian (computed separately) is not the same, the reason being different POS tagsets for the two languages used by TreeTagger. For Russian, a large amount of proper names were identified as common nouns, e.g. 'India', 'Mumbai', 'Hamas' etc. For German, these were identified as Named Entities.

Based on these observations, we compute the projection accuracy of each NP type as the number of correct markables of this type divided by the total number of projected markables of the same type. Table 5 shows the projection accuracy for both settings. According to these results, in the knowledge-lean approach, NPs are the less reliable projected type for German as compared to Named Entities, which is due to the fact that most of them lose their determiners at the alignment stage. For Russian, both NPs and Named Entities show similar results of over 80% with the `u-int` method. With the `u-con` method, all the scores are a bit lower due to lower Precision obtained by concatenation. As one can see from columns 3 and 4, it is possible to significantly improve the NP identification accuracy for German by using only a mention extractor: over 17% for both methods. However, this is not the case for Russian, where NP extraction relying on word alignment does not produce that much noise: the improvement is around 0.5-2.8%.

Pronouns exhibit the best projection accuracy for both languages. For German, the highest scores are achieved by the projection of possessive (97.1), personal (95.1) and relative (81.8) pronouns. Demonstrative pronouns show the lowest score (50.0) due to their scarcity in the gold and projected data. In setting 2, we can only achieve little improvement for different pronoun types, except for personal pronouns for German that exhibit lower accuracy.

These results explain the better projection quality when projecting to Russian as compared to projecting to German, since all the projected types show fair projection accuracy. Conversely, German NPs show poorer accuracy, while constituting almost one third of all the projected markables, which inevitably leads to lower Precision and Recall scores.

Evaluation by mention length (`u-int`). Finally, we compare mentions according to the number of tokens they consist of. Fig. 2a and Fig. 2b show the overall amount of tokens and the number of correct tokens of this length for German and Russian respectively in the `u-int` setting, in which higher Precision results were achieved. For German, the number of correct mentions gradually decreases up to the length of 5; after that, only one or no correct mentions are to be found in the target annotations. For Russian, the situation is almost the same, except for the mentions with length of 3, which are mostly incorrect.

[10] http://www.cis.uni-muenchen.de/ schmid/tools/TreeTagger/
[11] http://corpus.leeds.ac.uk/mocky/

	unify-int				u-con			
	→DE #	→DE %	→RU #	→RU %	→DE #	→DE %	→RU #	→RU %
NPs	146	29.6	286	58.8	264	28.4	450	52.2
Named Entities	145	29.4	26	0.05	245	26.3	53	6.2
Pronouns			113	23.3			237	27.5
-Personal pronouns	82	16.6	-	-	143	15.4	-	-
-Possessive pronouns	35	7.1	-	-	69	7.4	-	-
-Demonstrative pronouns	2	0.4	-	-	5	0.5	-	-
- Relative pronouns	11	2.2	-	-	12	1.3	-	-
Total	494	100	486	100	931	100	862	100

Table 4: Distribution of all projected markables by type for u-int and u-con methods

	u-int		u-con		u-int+*ment*		u-con+*ment*	
	→DE %	→RU %	→DE %	→RU %	→DE %	→RU %	→DE %	→RU %
NPs	53.4	82.5	53.0	77.8	72.0	85.3	70.1	78.3
Named Entities	91.0	92.3	82.0	88.7	95.2	92.3	84.1	88.7
Pronouns		92.0		89.9		92.9		90.3
Personal pronouns	95.1	-	95.1	-	87.8	-	92.3	-
Possessive pronouns	97.1	-	94.2	-	97.2	-	98.6	-
Demonstrative pronouns	50.0	-	40.0	-	100.0	-	40.0	-
Relative pronouns	81.8	-	83.3	-	100.0	-	100.0	-

Table 5: Projection accuracy for u-int and u-con methods

6 Discussion

Analysing the results for multi-source projection for both target languages, one can see that the scores achieved are quite comparable: the highest Precision of 83.7/85.8 for German/Russian and the highest Recall of 52.7 for both. Looking at the u-int method in setting 2, we still see that Precision is somewhat higher for Russian than for German (79.1 vs. 71.8 respectively). Overall, the best F1-scores for both languages are 57.0/59.0 German/Russian.

Importantly, for both target languages and in both settings, the multi-source projection results outperform the single-source results in terms of Precision or Recall; however, still not both simultaneously. In particular, the u-con method exhibits higher F1 scores as compared to single-source projection (55.0 vs. 57.0 for German and 58.8 vs. 59.0 for Russian).

As for the different projection methods, the results show that the balance between Precision and Recall scores is quite stable in both settings. In particular, concatenating mentions in overlapping chains (u-con) resulted in the most balanced Precision and Recall scores for both German and Russian. Furthermore, Precision can be improved in two ways: by taking the intersection of chains coming from two languages and by taking the intersection of mentions in the overlapping chains in two languages. While the first scenario is more unrealistic, leading to extremely low Recall numbers, the second scenario returns much better results in terms of both Precision and Recall.

Comparing our results to the most closely related work of Grishina and Stede (2015), we can see a large improvement in the projection quality for English-German in terms of both Precision and Recall already in the knowledge-lean setting: best Precision of 72.2 vs. 78.4/53.4 news/stories[12] respectively, and best Recall of 46.5 vs. 41.4/45.9. In setting 2, the results are even better: 83.7 and 57.0. As for Russian, we conclude that the multi-source approach leads to a slight improvement of projection results in terms of Precision (best Precision of 85.8 for settings 1,2 vs. 73.9/84.6), but not in terms of Recall (52.4 for setting 1 and 52.7 for setting 2 vs. 58.3/59.0), which is also due to the fact that the single-source projection performed slightly worse in the absence of intersective alignments.

Interestingly, the results for single-source projection also show that different directions of projection are not equally good: Projection from English still shows the best results, while Projection from German to Russian and from Russian to German exhibit much lower F1 numbers. In our opinion, the fact that projection results with language other than English as source are much lower had a negative impact on the multi-source projection, since adding lower-quality annotations

[12]Mind that stories constitute 30% of the corpus, therefore we consider our overall results higher.

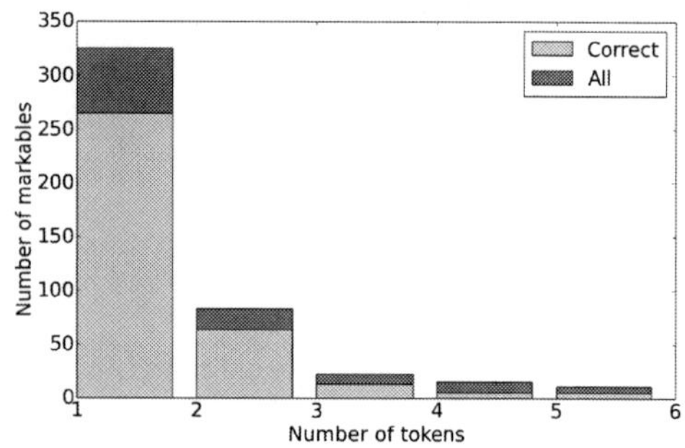

(a) German

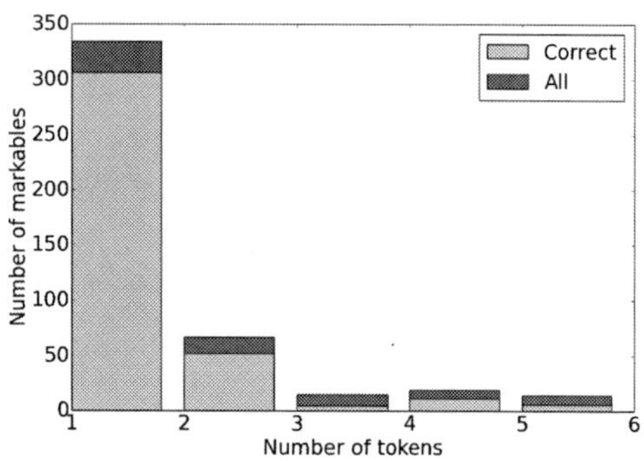

(b) Russian

Figure 2: Overall number of mentions and the number of correct mentions according to the number of tokens

leads to a decrease in both Precision and Recall scores. Therefore, concatenation of the two projections with one of them being of lower quality results in a slight drop in Precision and does not improve the Recall numbers significantly. Using projections of similar quality and more languages would result in better overall scores.

Automatic mention extraction and the mapping of target mentions to the extracted mentions to a high degree supported the identification of mentions and hence coreference scores for the English-German language pair. For Russian, conversely, this method only helped to a small extent, the reason being already high Precision scores achieved by projecting through word alignment. The qualitative analysis has shown that incorrectly identified mentions were of wrong part-of-speech (e.g. verbs, therefore it was not possible to map them to the automatically extracted mentions) or were no markables in the gold annotations.

In sum, our results have shown that projecting from two sources rather than one helps both to improve Precision and Recall. However, improving Precision appears to be an easier task than improving Recall. Achieving higher Recall seems to be a more difficult and expensive task as compared to eliminating noisy alignments and ensuring correct mention boundaries. If a potential target mention is absent on the source sides, it can hardly be recovered in the resulting annotations.

7 Conclusions

In this work, we examined the multi-source approach to projecting coreference annotations in a low-resource and a more linguistically-informed setting by implementing a direct projection algorithm and several methods for combining annotations coming from two sources. Comparing our results to a single-source approach, we observed that the former is able to outperform the latter one, both in terms of Precision and Recall. Specifically, our results suggest that the concatenation of coreference chains coming from two sources exhibits the highest balanced Precision and Recall scores, while the intersection helps to achieve the highest Precision.

We further analyzed the errors both quantitatively and qualitatively, focusing on the nature of the projected chains coming from both languages and the projection accuracy of different coreference mention types. Our results showed that noun phrases are more challenging for the projection algorithm than pronouns, and, as a by-product, we found that using automatic mention extraction to a large extent supports the recovery of target markables expressed by common noun phrases for German. However, this is not necessarily the case for Russian, for which using higher quality word alignments is more effective.

Having tested and assessed several methods of two-source annotation projection, we envision our future work on automatic annotation transfer in combining annotations coming from more than two source languages. Furthermore, we are interested in adapting a similar approach for projecting automatic annotations, which, in our opinion, could support the creation of a large-scale coreference corpus, suitable for the training of coreference resolvers in new languages.

References

Alan Akbik, Laura Chiticariu, Marina Danilevsky, Yunyao Li, Shivakumar Vaithyanathan, and Huaiyu

Zhu. 2015. Generating high quality proposition banks for multilingual semantic role labeling. In *Proceedings of the 53rd Annual Meeting of the Association for Computational Linguistics and the 7th International Joint Conference on Natural Language Processing (Volume 1: Long Papers)*, pages 397–407, Beijing, China, July. Association for Computational Linguistics.

Bernd Bohnet. 2010. Very high accuracy and fast dependency parsing is not a contradiction. In *Proceedings of the 23rd international conference on computational linguistics*, pages 89–97. Association for Computational Linguistics.

Yulia Grishina and Manfred Stede. 2015. Knowledge-lean projection of coreference chains across languages. In *Proceedings of the Eighth Workshop on Building and Using Comparable Corpora*, pages 14–22, Beijing, China, July. Association for Computational Linguistics.

Yulia Grishina and Manfred Stede, 2016. *Parallel coreference annotation guidelines*. Unpublished Manuscript[13].

Anders Johannsen, Željko Agić, and Anders Søgaard. 2016. Joint part-of-speech and dependency projection from multiple sources. In *Proceedings of the 54th Annual Meeting of the Association for Computational Linguistics (Volume 2: Short Papers)*, pages 561–566, Berlin, Germany, August. Association for Computational Linguistics.

Ophélie Lacroix, Lauriane Aufrant, Guillaume Wisniewski, and François Yvon. 2016. Frustratingly easy cross-lingual transfer for transition-based dependency parsing. In *Proceedings of the 2016 Conference of the North American Chapter of the Association for Computational Linguistics: Human Language Technologies*, pages 1058–1063, San Diego, California, June. Association for Computational Linguistics.

André F. T. Martins. 2015. Transferring coreference resolvers with posterior regularization. In *Proceedings of the 53rd Annual Meeting of the Association for Computational Linguistics and the 7th International Joint Conference on Natural Language Processing (Volume 1: Long Papers)*, pages 1427–1437, Beijing, China, July. Association for Computational Linguistics.

Joakim Nivre, Johan Hall, and Jens Nilsson. Maltparser: A data-driven parser-generator for dependency parsing. In *Proceedings of 5th international conference on Language Resources and Evaluation (LREC)*.

Franz Josef Och and Hermann Ney. 2003. A systematic comparison of various statistical alignment models. *Computational Linguistics*, 29(1):19–51.

[13]Available at https://github.com/yuliagrishina/CORBON-2017-Shared-Task/blob/master/Parallel_annotation_guidelines.pdf

Maciej Ogrodniczuk. 2013. Translation-and projection-based unsupervised coreference resolution for Polish. In *Language Processing and Intelligent Information Systems*, pages 125–130. Springer.

Oana Postolache, Dan Cristea, and Constantin Orasan. 2006. Transferring coreference chains through word alignment. In *Proceedings of 5th international conference on Language Resources and Evaluation (LREC)*.

Sameer S. Pradhan and Nianwen Xue. 2009. Ontonotes: The 90% solution. In *Proceedings of Human Language Technologies: The 2009 Annual Conference of the North American Chapter of the Association for Computational Linguistics, Companion Volume: Tutorial Abstracts*, pages 11–12, Boulder, Colorado, May. Association for Computational Linguistics.

Sameer Pradhan, Alessandro Moschitti, Nianwen Xue, Olga Uryupina, and Yuchen Zhang. 2012. CoNLL-2012 Shared Task: Modeling Multilingual Unrestricted Coreference in OntoNotes. In *Joint Conference on EMNLP and CoNLL - Shared Task*, pages 1–40, Jeju Island, Korea, July. Association for Computational Linguistics.

Altaf Rahman and Vincent Ng. 2012. Translation-based projection for multilingual coreference resolution. In *Proceedings of the 2012 Conference of the North American Chapter of the Association for Computational Linguistics: Human Language Technologies*, pages 720–730. Association for Computational Linguistics.

Mohammad Sadegh Rasooli and Michael Collins. 2015. Density-driven cross-lingual transfer of dependency parsers. In *Proceedings of the 2015 Conference on Empirical Methods in Natural Language Processing*, pages 328–338. Association for Computational Linguistics.

Helmut Schmid. 1995. Probabilistic part-of-speech tagging using decision trees. In *Proceedings of the ACL SIGDAT-Workshop*. Association for Computational Linguistics.

Serge Sharoff and Joakim Nivre. 2011. The proper place of men and machines in language technology: Processing russian without any linguistic knowledge. In *Proc. Dialogue 2011, Russian Conference on Computational Linguistics*.

José Guilherme Camargo Souza and Constantin Orăsan. 2011. Can projected chains in parallel corpora help coreference resolution? In *Discourse Anaphora and Anaphor Resolution Colloquium*, pages 59–69. Springer.

Sam Wiseman, Alexander M. Rush, and Stuart M. Shieber. 2016. Learning global features for coreference resolution. In *Proceedings of the 2016 Conference of the North American Chapter of the Association for Computational Linguistics: Human Language Technologies*, pages 994–1004, San

Diego, California, June. Association for Computational Linguistics.

David Yarowsky, Grace Ngai, and Richard Wicentowski. 2001. Inducing multilingual text analysis tools via robust projection across aligned corpora. In *Proceedings of the first international conference on Human language technology research*, pages 1–8. Association for Computational Linguistics.

CORBON 2017 Shared Task: Projection-Based Coreference Resolution

Yulia Grishina
Applied Computational Linguistics
FSP Cognitive Science
University of Potsdam
grishina@uni-potsdam.de

Abstract

The CORBON 2017 Shared Task, organised as part of the Coreference Resolution Beyond OntoNotes workshop at EACL 2017, presented a new challenge for multilingual coreference resolution: we offer a projection-based setting in which one is supposed to build a coreference resolver for a new language exploiting little or even no knowledge of it, with our languages of interest being German and Russian. We additionally offer a more traditional setting, targeting the development of a multilingual coreference resolver without any restrictions on the resources and methods used. In this paper, we describe the task setting and provide the results of one participant who successfully completed the task, comparing their results to the closely related previous research. Analysing the task setting and the results, we discuss the major challenges and make suggestions on the future directions of coreference evaluation.

1 Motivation

High-quality coreference resolution plays an important role in many NLP applications. However, developing a coreference resolver for a new language requires extensive world knowledge as well as annotated resources, which are usually expensive to create. Previous shared tasks on multilingual coreference resolution, such as the SemEval 2010 shared task on Coreference Resolution in Multiple Languages (Recasens et al., 2010) and the CoNLL 2012 shared task on Modeling Multilingual Unrestricted Coreference in OntoNotes (Pradhan et al., 2012), operated in a setting where a large amount of training data was provided to train coreference resolvers in a fully supervised manner. Our shared task has a different goal: We are primarily interested in a low-resource setting. In particular, we seek to investigate how well one can build a coreference resolver for a language for which there is no coreference-annotated data available for training.

With a rising interest in annotation projection, we focused on a projection-based task, which, in our opinion, could facilitate the application of existing coreference resolution algorithms to new languages. Annotation projection is a technique which allows us to automatically transfer annotations from a well-studied, typically resource-rich language to a low-resource language across parallel corpora. It was first introduced in the pioneering work of Yarowsky et al. (2001), who exploited annotation projection to induce POS taggers, NP chunkers and morphological analysers for several languages. Their approach is illustrated in Fig. 1, which shows automatic transfer of POS tags from English to French via word alignment. Thereafter, annotation projection was successfully applied for different NLP tasks, including coreference resolution (Postolache et al., 2006; Rahman and Ng, 2012; Grishina and Stede, 2015; Martins, 2015).

In the shared task, the participants were offered an automatically labelled source language corpus, which could be used to automatically transfer the annotations to the target side and subsequently train a new system. With English typically being the most well-studied and resource-rich language, we employed it as our source language. To verify the applicability of our projection-based approach to two different languages, we chose German and Russian as our target languages. We believe that, with this exciting setting, the shared task could help promote the development of coreference technologies that are applicable to a larger number of natural languages than is currently possible. In order to test the limitations of our approach and for a fair comparison, we also offered

Proceedings of the 2nd Workshop on Coreference Resolution Beyond OntoNotes (CORBON 2017), co-located with EACL 2017, pages 51–55,
Valencia, Spain, April 4, 2017.

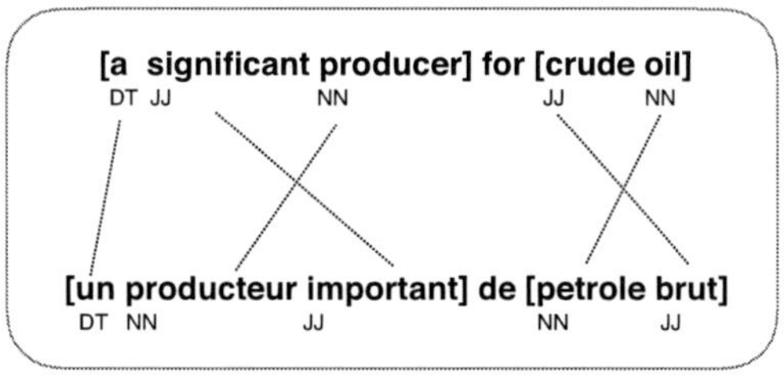

Figure 1: Direct projection algorithm by Yarowsky et al. (2001)

the participants a more traditional setting, where one was supposed to develop a multilingual coreference resolver with no restriction on the resources and methods used.

The paper is structured as follows. Section 2 gives a detailed overview of the task setting. Section 3 describes the participating system and the evaluation results. In Section 4, we analyse the results and compare them to the related work on the topic. Finally, Section 5 presents conclusions.

2 Task setting

The main goal of the CORBON 2017 Shared Task was the evaluation of multilingual coreference resolution in a low-resource scenario. Furthermore, we introduced an open setting in which we did not impose any restrictions on the resources and methods used by the participants in the development of their systems. In sum, the participants competed in two tracks:

- **Closed track:** coreference resolution on German and Russian using annotation projection. In this setting, the participants were allowed to use the English part of the OntoNotes corpus (Hovy et al., 2006) to train a source coreference resolver, or they could use any of the publicly-available coreference resolvers trained on the same data. They could then use whatever parallel corpus and method they prefer to project the English annotations into German/Russian and subsequently train a new coreference resolver on the projected annotations. As for additional linguistic information, the participants could use POS information provided by the parser of their choice.

- **Open track:** coreference resolution on German and Russian with no restriction on the kind of coreference-annotated data the participants can use for training. For instance, they could label their own German/Russian coreference data and use it to train a German/Russian coreference resolver, or adopt a heuristic-based approach where they employ knowledge of German/Russian to write coreference rules for these languages.

Since our main focus was on the low-resource setting, we did not provide any German or Russian manually coreference-annotated data to the participants. Instead, to facilitate system development in the closed setting, the shared task participants were provided an English-German and English-Russian parallel corpora as a training set. Specifically, we chose the English-German and English-Russian parts of the News-Commentary11 parallel corpus[1] taken from the OPUS collection of parallel corpora (Tiedemann, 2012).

The original sentence-aligned text files were split into documents and tokenised using EuroParl tools[2] (Koehn, 2005). The English side of the corpora was labelled automatically using the Berkeley Entity Resolution system (Durrett and Klein, 2014), which was trained on the English part of the OntoNotes corpus (Hovy et al., 2006).

Furthermore, in this setting, the participants were allowed to use other existing parallel texts processed in a similar manner. In the open track, there was no restriction on the data used for system training.

As for the test set, we chose the English-German-Russian parallel corpus described in Grishina and Stede (2015). The guidelines used for the annotation of the corpus are quite compatible with the OntoNotes guidelines for English (Version 6.0) in terms of the types of referring expressions that are annotated (Grishina and Stede, 2016). The exceptions are that they (a) handle only NPs and do not annotate verbs that are coreferent with NPs, (b) include appositions into the markable span and do not mark them as a separate relation, (c) mark relative pronouns as markables, and (d) annotate pronominal adverbs in German if they co-refer with an NP. A sample of the German and Russian annotations was provided to the participants to support their system development. The size of the training and test datasets are presented

[1] http://opus.lingfil.uu.se/News-Commentary11.php

[2] http://www.statmt.org/europarl/

	Training set			Test set		
	#docs	#sents	#tokens	#docs	#sents	#tokens
English	5749	221 844	5 341 828	–	–	–
German	5749	221 844	5 404 568	10	413	8753
English	4869	188 761	4 503 260	–	–	–
Russian	4869	188 761	4 290 891	10	413	8092

Table 1: Size of the training and test datasets

System	closed track German	closed track Russian	official score
CUNI	29.40	30.94	**30.17**

Table 2: Official CORBON 2017 Shared Task results

in Table 1.

The evaluation of the results was conducted in a similar way as in the CoNLL 2012 shared task (Pradhan et al., 2012). We employed three commonly-used scoring metrics | MUC, B-CUBED and CEAF$_e$ | and took the unweighted average of these scores (as computed by the official CoNLL 2012 scorer[3]) to determine the winning system. We did not evaluate singletons and therefore asked the participants to exclude them from their results prior to the submission.

3 CORBON 2017 systems and results

Out of several candidates, only one team successfully completed the task and submitted their results during the official evaluation period. This team consisted of Michal Novák, Anna Nedoluzhko and Zdenek Zabokrtský from Charles University in Prague, Czech Republic. They submitted their results for the closed track, with the following system description:

- **CUNI:** The system submitted by Charles University (CUNI) is a projection-based coreference resolver for German and Russian. It is trained exclusively on coreference relations projected through a parallel corpus from English. The authors used the training corpus and automatic annotation of English coreference as provided by the shared task organizers. Their resolver makes use of multiple models, and each of them addresses a specific anaphoric mention type individually. Furthermore, it operates on the level of deep syntax. The original surface representation of coreference thus must be transferred to this level. Analogously, coreference relations found by their system must be in the end transformed back to the surface representation, in order to be evaluated in accordance with the task's requirements.

The system was assessed by computing the official CoNLL 2012 metric as described above, and the results of the shared task are presented in Table 2.

4 Discussion

The team from Charles University made an important contribution to the task of exploring annotation projection for multilingual coreference resolution. Of particular importance is the development of a projection-based coreference resolver for Russian, which is an under-resourced language in terms of coreference resolution.

The CUNI system achieved CoNLL scores of 29.40 and 30.94 for the German and Russian portions of the official evaluation dataset, respectively. As the authors themselves acknowledge, the model ablation analysis of their system showed that the models for third-person personal and possessive pronouns and NPs contributed the most to overall performance.

The analysis of the resolver's stages showed that while for Russian the resolver trained on the annotations projected from English achieves 66% of the quality achieved by the English resolver (CoNLL score), this number drops to 46% for German (Novák et al., 2017).

A more detailed analysis of Precision and Recall scores showed that, on one hand, the system was able to achieve relatively high average Precision scores[4] (62.5 and 59.56 for German and Russian, respectively). On the other hand, average Re-

[3]https://github.com/conll/reference-coreference-scorers

[4]Average Precision and Recall scores are computed as an unweighted average of MUC, B-CUBED and CEAF Precision and Recall respectively.

call numbers for both languages are considerably lower: 20.3 for German and 21.2 for Russian.

Since it was not possible to compare their results to those obtained in a similar setting, we briefly compare them to the most closely related work on annotation projection for coreference resolution. Firstly, we consider the experimental evaluation of projection method quality conducted by Grishina and Stede (2015) on the same dataset using gold annotations (without system training). Grishina and Stede's results exhibited a similar balance between Precision and Recall scores, where a higher Precision was accompanied by a comparatively lower Recall (P=68.0/82.1 and R=45.8/62.6 for German/Russian). Furthermore, we look at two related studies by Souza and Orăsan (2011) and Martins (2015), who also experimented with cross-lingual training on different languages and datasets, but in a similar projection-based setting. While the former fails to beat a simple baseline that clusters together mentions with the same head[5], the latter achieves F1 scores of 38.82 for Spanish and 37.23 for Portuguese. These performance numbers are slightly higher than the corresponding results for German and Russian.

In sum, the results of the shared task show that a projection-based approach applied to coreference resolution can support creating coreference resolvers even if no manually annotated data is available. In particular, this approach is already able to achieve promising Precision scores, thus providing coreference-annotated data of fair quality. However, the coverage of the projected annotations still requires improvement, which, in our view, could be achieved by using, for instance, a bilingual dictionary or automatically induced paraphrases in order to retrieve missing coreference mentions on the target side.

Another way to improve Recall could be to increase the robustness of mention detection by using multiple source annotations. Specifically, if a coreference mention is absent in the first source language and therefore cannot be projected, it could still be recovered by another source language.[6] Furthermore, the choice of the source language(s) in respect to the target language is also an interesting factor that influences the projection results; however, this issue needs to be investigated further by comparing the quality of a projection approach for different languages in the same setting.

5 Conclusions

In this paper, we presented the CORBON 2017 Shared Task, the first evaluation task on projection-based coreference resolution. The novelty of this task is that it did not provide any manually annotated gold data as the training set, but relied solely upon the automatic annotations obtained by using a state-of-the-art English coreference resolver. The results of the task show that, in this low-resource setting, it is possible to build a new resolver for two different languages with reasonably high Precision scores. Therefore, we conclude that this task can be seen as a fair starting point for projection-based multilingual coreference resolution.

Overall, we believe that this task has successfully continued the important tradition of evaluating state-of-the art coreference systems. Moreover, we hope that it will bring more interest to the task of cross-lingual coreference resolution and will hopefully contribute to the future progress of our field.

The complete data package for the shared task was made available via `https://github.com/yuliagrishina/CORBON-2017-Shared-Task`.

Acknowledgements

The shared task coordinator would like to thank CORBON 2017 workshop organisers – Vincent Ng and Maciej Ogrodniczuk – for providing continuous support and sharing their insights throughout the whole organisation process.

References

Greg Durrett and Dan Klein. 2014. A joint model for entity analysis: Coreference, typing, and linking. In *Transactions of the Association for Computational Linguistics*.

Yulia Grishina and Manfred Stede. 2015. Knowledge-lean projection of coreference chains across languages. In *Proceedings of the 8th Workshop on Building and Using Comparable Corpora, Beijing, China*, page 14. Association for Computational Linguistics.

[5]Probably due to erroneous annotations on the source side, as the authors themselves acknowledge.

[6]However, combining coreference annotations coming from several sources is not a trivial task, as shown in Grishina and Stede (2017).

Yulia Grishina and Manfred Stede, 2016. *Parallel coreference annotation guidelines*. Unpublished manuscript.

Yulia Grishina and Manfred Stede. 2017. Multi-source annotation projection of coreference chains: assessing strategies and testing opportunities. In *Proceedings of the 2nd Workshop on Coreference Resolution Beyond OntoNotes (CORBON)*, Valencia, Spain, April. Association for Computational Linguistics.

Eduard Hovy, Mitchell Marcus, Martha Palmer, Lance Ramshaw, and Ralph Weischedel. 2006. OntoNotes: the 90% solution. In *Proceedings of the human language technology conference of the NAACL, Companion Volume: Short Papers*, pages 57–60. Association for Computational Linguistics.

Philipp Koehn. 2005. Europarl: A parallel corpus for statistical machine translation. In *MT summit*, volume 5, pages 79–86.

André F. T. Martins. 2015. Transferring coreference resolvers with posterior regularization. In *Proceedings of the 53rd Annual Meeting of the Association for Computational Linguistics and the 7th International Joint Conference on Natural Language Processing (Volume 1: Long Papers)*, pages 1427–1437, Beijing, China, July. Association for Computational Linguistics.

Michal Novák, Anna Nedoluzhko, and Zdenek Zabokrtský. 2017. Projection-based coreference resolution using deep syntax. In *Proceedings of the 2nd Workshop on Coreference Resolution Beyond OntoNotes (CORBON), Valencia, Spain*. Association for Computational Linguistics.

Oana Postolache, Dan Cristea, and Constantin Orasan. 2006. Transferring coreference chains through word alignment. In *Proceedings of 5th international conference on Language Resources and Evaluation (LREC)*.

Sameer Pradhan, Alessandro Moschitti, Nianwen Xue, Olga Uryupina, and Yuchen Zhang. 2012. CoNLL-2012 shared task: Modeling multilingual unrestricted coreference in OntoNotes. In *Joint Conference on EMNLP and CoNLL-Shared Task*, pages 1–40. Association for Computational Linguistics.

Altaf Rahman and Vincent Ng. 2012. Translation-based projection for multilingual coreference resolution. In *Proceedings of the 2012 Conference of the North American Chapter of the Association for Computational Linguistics: Human Language Technologies*, pages 720–730. Association for Computational Linguistics.

Marta Recasens, Lluís Màrquez, Emili Sapena, M Antònia Martí, Mariona Taulé, Véronique Hoste, Massimo Poesio, and Yannick Versley. 2010. SemEval-2010 Task 1: Coreference resolution in multiple languages. In *Proceedings of the 5th International Workshop on Semantic Evaluation*, pages 1–8. Association for Computational Linguistics.

José Guilherme Camargo Souza and Constantin Orăsan. 2011. Can projected chains in parallel corpora help coreference resolution? In *Discourse Anaphora and Anaphor Resolution Colloquium*, pages 59–69. Springer.

Jörg Tiedemann. 2012. Parallel data, tools and interfaces in OPUS. In *Proceedings of 8th international conference on Language Resources and Evaluation (LREC)*, pages 2214–2218.

David Yarowsky, Grace Ngai, and Richard Wicentowski. 2001. Inducing multilingual text analysis tools via robust projection across aligned corpora. In *Proceedings of the first international conference on Human language technology research*, pages 1–8. Association for Computational Linguistics.

Projection-based Coreference Resolution Using Deep Syntax

Michal Novák and **Anna Nedoluzhko** and **Zdeněk Žabokrtský**
Charles University, Faculty of Mathematics and Physics
Institute of Formal and Applied Linguistics
Malostranské náměstí 25, CZ-11800 Prague 1
{mnovak,nedoluzko,zabokrtsky}@ufal.mff.cuni.cz

Abstract

The paper describes the system for coreference resolution in German and Russian, trained exclusively on coreference relations projected through a parallel corpus from English. The resolver operates on the level of deep syntax and makes use of multiple specialized models. It achieves 32 and 22 points in terms of CoNLL score for Russian and German, respectively. Analysis of the evaluation results show that the resolver for Russian is able to preserve 66% of the English resolver's quality in terms of CoNLL score. The system was submitted to the Closed track of the CORBON 2017 Shared task.

1 Introduction

Projection techniques in parallel corpora are a popular choice to obtain annotation of various linguistic phenomena in a resource-poor language. No tools or gold manual labels are required for this language. Instead, far more easily available parallel corpora are used as a means to transfer the labels to this language from a language, for which such a tool or manual annotation exists.

This paper presents a system submitted to the closed track of the shared task collocated with the Workshop on Coreference Resolution Beyond OntoNotes (CORBON 2017).[1] The task was to build coreference resolution systems for German and Russian without coreference-annotated training data in these languages. The only allowed coreference-annotated training data was the English part of the OntoNotes corpus (Pradhan et al., 2013). Alternatively, any publicly available resolution tool trained on this corpora could be employed.

We adopted and slightly modified an approach previously used by de Souza and Orăsan (2011) and Martins (2015). Parallel English-German and English-Russian corpora are used to project coreference links that had been automatically resolved on the English side of the corpora. The projected links then serve as input data for training a resolver. Unlike the previous works, our coreference resolution system operates on a level of deep syntax. The original surface representation of coreference thus must be transferred to this level. Likewise, coreference relations found by our system must be in the end transformed back to the surface representation, so that they can be evaluated in accordance with the task's requirements. Our resolver also takes advantage of multiple models, each of them targeting a specific mention type.

According to the official results, we were the only participating team. Our system achieved 29.40 points and 30.94 points of CoNLL score for German and Russian portion of the official evaluation dataset, respectively.

The paper is structured as follows. After introducing related works in Section 2, the paper continues with description of the system and its three main stages (Section 3). Section 4 lists the training and testing data to enable evaluation of the proposed system in Section 5. In Section 6, the resolver is analyzed using two different methods. Finally, we conclude in Section 7.

2 Related Work

Approaches of cross-lingual projection have received attention with the advent of parallel corpora. They are usually aimed to bridge the gap of missing resources in the target language. So far, they have been quite successfully applied to

[1] Details on the shared task are available in its overview paper (Grishina, 2017) and at http://corbon.nlp.ipipan.waw.pl/index.php/shared-task/

Proceedings of the 2nd Workshop on Coreference Resolution Beyond OntoNotes (CORBON 2017), co-located with EACL 2017, pages 56–64,
Valencia, Spain, April 4, 2017.

part-of-speech tagging (Täckström et al., 2013), syntactic parsing (Hwa et al., 2005), semantic role labeling (Padó and Lapata, 2009), opinion mining (Almeida et al., 2015), etc. Coreference resolution is no exception in this respect.

Coreference projection is generally approached in two ways. They differ in how they obtain the translation to the language for which a coreference resolver exits. The first approach applies a machine-translation service to create synthetic data in this language. This usually happens at test times on previously unseen texts. Such approach was used by Rahman and Ng (2012) on Spanish and Italian, and by Ogrodniczuk (2013) on Polish.

The other approach, which we employ in this work, takes advantage of the human-translated parallel corpus of the two languages. Unlike the first approach, the translation must be provided already in train time. Postolache et al. (2006) followed this approach using an English-Romanian corpus. They projected manually annotated coreference, which was then postprocessed by linguists to acquire high quality annotation in Romanian. de Souza and Orăsan (2011) applied projection in a parallel English-Portuguese corpus to build a resolver for Portuguese. Our work practically follows this schema, differing in some design details (e.g., using specialized models, resolution on a level of deep syntax). Martins (2015) extended this approach by learning coreference with a specific type of regularization at the end. Their gains over the standard projection come from ability of their method to recover links missing due to projection over inaccurate alignment.

3 System description

Our system for coreference resolution is an example of the projection in parallel corpus. It requires a corpus of parallel sentences in a source (English) and a target language (German and Russian). The procedure consists of three stages illustrated in Figure 1. First, coreference links on the source-language side of the corpus are automatically resolved (see Section 3.1). The acquired links are then projected to the target-language side (Section 3.2). Finally, the target-language side enriched with the projected links is used as a training data to build a coreference resolver (Section 3.3).

3.1 Coreference relations in English

The source-language side of the parallel corpus must get labeled with coreference. In our case, the English side of the parallel corpus already contained annotation of coreference provided by the shared task's organizers. The annotation is obtained by Berkeley Entity Resolution system (Durrett and Klein, 2014), trained on the English section of OntoNotes 5.0 (Pradhan et al., 2013).

Although Berkeley system is a state-of-the-art performing coreference resolver, we found that it rarely addresses relative and demonstrative pronouns. To label coreference for relative pronouns, we introduced a module from the Treex framework[2] that employs a simple heuristics based on syntactic trees. Coreference of demonstratives has not been further resolved.

3.2 Cross-lingual projection of coreference

The second stage the proposed schema is to project coreference relations from the source-language to the target-language side of the parallel corpus.

Specifically, we make use of word-level alignment, which allows for potentially more accurate projection. As the parallel data provided for the task are aligned only on the sentence level, word alignment must be acquired on our own. For this purpose, we used GIZA++ (Och and Ney, 2000) a tool particularly popular in the community of statistical machine translation. Even though GIZA++ implements a fully unsupervised approach, which allows for easy extension of the training data with raw parallel texts, it did not prove to be useful for us. We thus obtained word alignment for both the language pairs by running the tool solely on the parallel corpora coming from the organizers.[3]

Since both German and Russian are morphologically rich languages, we expected word alignment to work better on lemmatized texts. We applied TreeTagger (Schmid, 1995), and MATE tools (Björkelund et al., 2010) for lemmatization in Russian and German, respectively. For robustness, also English texts were preprocessed with a similar procedure, namely a rule-based lemmati-

[2]Treex (Popel and Žabokrtský, 2010) is a modular NLP framework, primarily designed for machine translation over deep syntax layer. It contains numerous modules for analysis in multiple languages.

[3]This deserves more experiments with collections of additional data of varying sizes and different algorithms. Due to time reasons we did not manage to finish them, though.

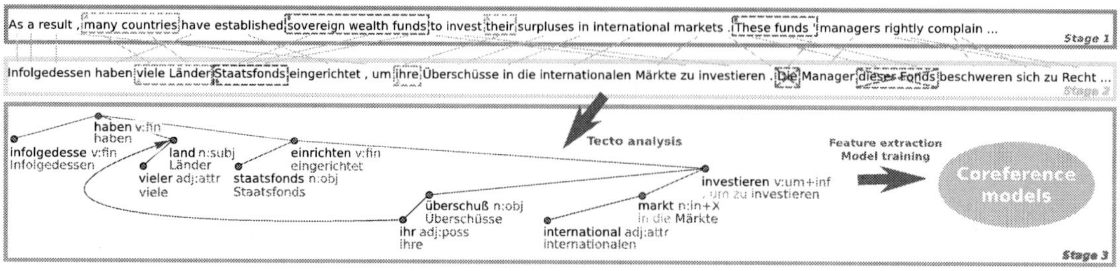

Figure 1: Architecture of the system that consists of three stages: coreference resolution in English (Stage 1), cross-lingual projection of coreference (Stage 2) and resolution in the target language (Stage 3). In the projection stage, the mention *These funds'* is not projected because it is aligned to a discontinuous German span.

zation available as a module in the Treex framework.

Based on the word alignment, the projection itself works as shown in Figure 1. We project mention spans along with its entity identifiers, which are shared among the cluster of coreferential mentions. Only such a mention is projected, whose counterpart forms a consecutive sequence of tokens in the target-language text. In practice, this approach succeeds in projecting around 90% of mentions.[4]

3.3 Coreference resolution in German and Russian

At this point, projected links are ready to serve as training data for a coreference resolver. We make use of an updated version of the already existing resolver implemented within the Treex framework, which operates on a level of deep syntax. All the texts must thus be analyzed and the projected mentions must be transferred up to this level before being used for training.

Analysis up to the tectogrammatical layer. Treex coreference resolver operates on a level of deep syntax, in Prague theory (Sgall et al., 1986) called tectogrammatical layer. On this layer, a sentence is represented as a dependency tree. Compared to a standard surface dependency tree, the tectogrammatical one is more compact as it consists only of content words (see Figure 1). In addition, several types of ellipsis can be reconstructed in the tree, e.g. pro-drops.

To transform a text in a target language from a surface form to a tectogrammatical representation, we processed it with the following pipelines:

[4]However, they do not need to be necessarily correct, as the alignment may contain errors.

German texts are processed with the MATE tools pipeline (Björkelund et al., 2010) that includes lemmatization, part-of-speech tagging, and transition-based dependency parsing (Bohnet and Nivre, 2012; Seeker and Kuhn, 2012). The surface dependency tree is then converted to the Prague style of annotation using a converter from the HamleDT project (Zeman et al., 2014). Transformation to tectogrammatics is then performed by a general Treex pipeline, with some language-dependent adjustments.

Russian texts are being parsed directly to the Prague style of surface dependency tree. We trained a UDPipe tool (Straka et al., 2016) on data from SynTagRus corpus (Boguslavsky et al., 2000) converted to the Prague style within the HamleDT project.[5] Although UDPipe trained on this data is able to lemmatize, we used lemmas produced by TreeTagger instead, as they seemed to be of better quality. In the same fashion as for German, tectogrammatical tree is built from the surface dependency tree using the Treex pipeline adjusted to Russian.

We also included named entity recognition, namely NameTag tool (Straková et al., 2014), to the pipeline. We had trained it on an extended version of the Persons-1000 collection (Mozharova and Loukachevitch, 2016) and named entity annotation of the NoSta-D corpus (Benikova et al., 2014) for Russian and German, respectively.

Transfer of mentions from the surface and back. On the tectogrammatical layer, a corefer-

[5]We observed lower quality of the Russian parser compared to the German one. The author of UDPipe had instructed us to run the training several times with different values of hyperparameters. However, due to time reasons we ran the training only once, thus probably picking not the most optimal model.

ence link always connects two nodes that represent heads of the mentions. Tectogrammatics does not specify a span of the mention, though. The mention usually spans over the whole subtree, except for some notable cases. For instance, an antecedent of a relative pronoun does not include the relative clause itself in its span, even though the clause belongs to a subtree of the antecedent.

The transfer from the surface to the tectogrammatics is easy – a head of the mention must be found. We use the dependency structure of a tectogrammatical tree for this and out of all nodes representing nouns or pronouns contained in the mention we pick the one that is closest to the root of the tree.

In the opposite direction, we consider the whole tectogrammatical subtree of a coreferential node. As mentions observed in the datasets rarely include a dependent clause, we rather exclude all such clauses. We skip possible trailing punctuation and finally, we mark the first and the last token of such selection as boundaries of the mention. Due to strict rules to find a mention span and possibly scrambled syntactic parses, this transfer is prone to errors (see Section 6).

Specialized models and features. Treex resolver implements a mention-ranking approach (Denis and Baldridge, 2007). In other words, every candidate mention forms an instance, aggregating all antecedent candidates from a predefined window of a surrounding context. The antecedent candidates are ranked and the one with the highest score is marked as the antecedent. Moreover, a dummy antecedent candidate is added. Highest score for the dummy antecedent implies that the candidate mention is not anaphoric, in fact.

In detail, the resolver consists of multiple models, each of them focused on a specific mention type, e.g., relative pronouns, demonstrative pronouns, or noun phrases. It makes possible to use different windows and different features for each of the types. Personal and possessive pronouns are addressed jointly by two models: a model for personal and possessive pronouns in third person and a model for these pronouns in other persons (in the following denoted as *PP3* and *PPo pronouns*, respectively). Model configurations shared for both languages are listed in Table 1.

Features exploit information collected during the analysis to the tectogrammatical layer. As seen in the table, our models are trained using two kinds

Mention type	DE	RU	Window	Featset
NP	✓	✓	5 prev sents curr sent, preceding	NP
PP3	✓	✓	1 prev sent curr sent, preceding	general
PPo	✓	✓		
demonstrative	✓	✓		
reflexive	✓	✓	curr sent, all	
reflexive possessive	×	✓		
relative	✓	✓	curr sent, preceding	

Table 1: Configuration of the coreference model for each mention type.

of a feature set:

- *General*: gender and number agreement, other morphological features, distance features, named entity types, syntactic patterns in tectogrammatical trees (to address e.g., relative and reflexive pronouns), dependency relations;
- *NP*: General + head lemma match, head lemma Levehnstein distance, full match; for German: + a similarity score based on word2vec (Mikolov et al., 2013) embeddings[6] of the mention heads.

The models were trained with logistic regression optimized by stochastic gradient descent. We varied different values of hyperparameters (e.g., number of passes over data, L1/L2 regularization) and picked the setting best performing on the DevAuto set (see Section 4). The learning method is implemented in the Vowpal Wabbit toolkit.[7]

4 Datasets

Raw datasets without manual annotation of coreference are used to train the pipeline described in Section 3. In contrast, manually annotated datasets are reserved exclusively for evaluation purposes. Table 2 shows some basic statistics of the datasets. We refer to each dataset by its label, which consists of two parts. The first part denotes the main purpose of the dataset: *Train* is used for training, *Dev* for development testing, and *Eval* for blind evaluation testing. The second part indicates the origin of the coreference annotation contained in the dataset: *Auto* denotes the projected automatic annotation, *Off* is the official manual annotation provided by the task's organizers, and *Add*

[6] http://devmount.github.io/GermanWordEmbeddings/

[7] https://github.com/JohnLangford/vowpal_wabbit/wiki

Dataset	# Doc.	# Sent.	# EN Tok.	# T Tok.
German				
TrainAuto	4,991	192k	4,834k	4,881k
DevAuto	400	15.4k	391k	395k
DevOff	1	35	–	1k
DevAdd	5	207	5.3k	5.4k
EvalOff	10	404	–	8.8k
Russian				
TrainAuto	3,991	155k	3,847k	3,669k
DevAuto	450	17.5k	436k	417k
DevOff	1	34	–	1k
DevAdd	5	207	5.3k	5.1k
EvalOff	10	412	–	8.1k

Table 2: Statistics of the datasets used throughout this work. The last two columns show the number of tokens in English and in the target language.

denotes the additional dataset annotated by the authors of this paper.

Raw data. We employed the parallel corpora provided by the task's organizers for building the resolver. Both the English-German and English-Russian corpora come from the *News-Commentary11* collection (Tiedemann, 2012). The datasets were provided in a tokenized sentence-aligned format. We split both corpora into two parts: *TrainAuto* and *DevAuto*. While the former is used for training the models, the latter serves to pick the best values of the learning method's hyperparameters (see Section 3.3).

Coreference-annotated data. For evaluation purposes, we used two datasets manually annotated with coreference: *DevOff* and *DevAdd*. Except for these datasets, a dataset for the final evaluation (*EvalOff*) of the shared task was provided by the organizer. However, the coreference annotation of this dataset has not been published.

Similarly to the raw data, DevOff has been provided by the task's organizers. In fact, both in German and Russian it is represented by a single monolingual document, presumably coming from the News-Commentary11 collection.

DevAdd dataset consists of the same five documents randomly selected from both the English-German and English-Russian parallel corpora so that none of these are included in TrainAuto. Coreference relations were annotated on all the three language sides. The Russian and English sides were labelled by one of this paper's co-authors, who speaks native Russian and fluent

Mention type	German		Russian	
	DevOff	**DevAdd**	**DevOff**	**DevAdd**
all	42/370	343/2003	54/497	312/2348
NP	27/312	181/1568	40/475	157/2129
PP3	10/ 16	76/ 142	10/ 10	68/ 70
PPo	0/ 4	33/ 53	1/ 2	29/ 49
demonstrative	1/ 19	9/ 107	0/ 4	0/ 27
reflexive	0/ 7	3/ 48	0/ 1	6/ 9
reflexive possessive	–	–	3/ 5	27/ 29
relative	4/ 12	41/ 85	0/ 0	25/ 35

Table 3: Distribution of mention types in German and Russian coreference-annotated datasets. Denominators show the number of all mention candidates while numerators only of the anaphoric ones.

English, and has long experience of annotating anaphoric relations. The German side was split among three annotators and their outputs were revised by the annotator of the Russian and English part to reach higher consistency. They all followed the annotation guideline published by the organizers.[8] The reason for creating additional annotated data is that the DevOff set consists only of a thousand words per language, which we found insufficient to reliably assess quality of designed systems. The English side was labelled to allow for assessing the quality of the projection pipeline over its stages (see Section 6).

Let us show some notable properties of the German and Russian evaluation data. Table 2 highlights that the DevAdd sets expectedly contain five times more words than their DevOff counterparts. However, the number of sentences is six times bigger. This may affect a proportion of individual mention types.

Table 3 gives a detailed picture of candidate and anaphoric mentions' counts. Whereas Russian anaphoric NPs account for 75% of all the anaphoric mentions in DevOff, it is only 50% in DevAdd. The disproportion appears also between the German datasets.

Finally, some of the mention types appear rarely in the DevOff sets. It especially holds for the Russian DevOff containing a lack of reflexive, relative and PPo pronouns. Conversely, some of the even well-populated types are rarely or never anaphoric (e.g., German demonstrative, reflexive and PPo pronouns).

[8] https://github.com/yuliagrishina/CORBON-2017-Shared-Task/blob/master/Parallel_annotation_guidelines.pdf

5 Evaluation

For both German and Russian, we submitted a single system to the shared task. Both the systems fulfill the requirements set on the closed track of the task. To build them we exploited the parallel English-German and English-Russian corpora selected from the News-Commentary11 collection by the task's organizers.

Metrics. We present the results in terms of four standard coreference measures: MUC (Vilain et al., 1995), B^3 (Bagga and Baldwin, 1998), CEAF-e (Luo, 2005) and the CoNLL score (Pradhan et al., 2014). The CoNLL score is an average of F-scores of the previous three measures. It was the main score of some previous coreference-related shared tasks, e.g., CoNLL 2012 (Pradhan et al., 2012), and it remains so for the CORBON 2017 Shared task.

Results. In Table 4, we report the results of evaluating the submitted systems. Comparison across languages shows very similar performance on the DevOff set. However, evaluation on the larger DevAdd set suggests the Russian resolver performs better. Scores on the *EvalOff* dataset confirms higher quality of the Russian resolver, however, the gap is not so big. As the latter dataset is the largest, these results can be considered the most reliable.

6 Discussion

We conducted two additional experiments to learn more about the properties of the projection system. The first experiment investigates the impact of models for individual mention types. The second experiment, in contrast, should tell us more about the quality of the system over its stages.

Model ablations. We conducted a model ablation experiment to shed more light on the model quality and difference between the two evaluation datasets. We repeated the same evaluation, however, each time with a model for a specified mention type left out.

Results in Table 5 show that models for PP3 pronouns and NPs are the most valuable. Better performance of the Russian resolver on DevAdd seems to partly result from a decent model for reflexive possessives, which do not exist in German. Other observations accord with what we highlighted above after inspecting datasets' statistics

Mention type	German		Russian	
	DevOff	DevAdd	DevOff	DevAdd
all	**24.2**	**22.4**	**24.2**	**31.8**
⊖ NP	-8.7	-4.6	-7.6	-3.0
⊖ PP3	-11.7	-11.3	-7.5	-10.4
⊖ PPo	+0.5	-1.0	0	-1.1
⊖ demonstrative	+0.5	-0.1	0	0
⊖ reflexive	0	0	0	0
⊖ reflexive possessive	–	–	-4.1	-6.4
⊖ relative	0	-1.9	0	-3.4

Table 5: Results of model ablation. The *all* line describes the complete resolver. Every following line represent an ablated resolver with a model for a given mention type left out. Differences in scores are listed in such line.

in Table 3. There is a big disproportion in score between the two datasets after the model for NPs is removed. This may be a consequence of different ratios of anaphoric NPs to all the anaphoric mentions. Multiple models seem to have marginal, zero, or even negative impact on the final performance. The reasons are threefold:

- low frequency of the mention type in DevOff (e.g., Russian relative and PPo pronouns);
- low frequency of its anaphoric occurrences in the dataset (e.g., all demonstrative pronouns, German reflexive and PPo pronouns)
- the model learned to label most candidates as non-anaphoric (e.g. German demonstrative and reflexive pronouns)

Performance over projection stages. The final performance about 20-30 points seems to be much worse than the CoNLL scores over 60 points observed at the CoNLL 2012 shared task for English. Is coreference resolution in German and Russian so difficult or the projection system deteriorates as it proceeds over its stages?

To answer these questions, we evaluated the output of four stages of the projection CR system. First, we scored the original automatic coreference annotation provided by the Berkeley resolver and the Treex resolver for relative pronouns. This tells us the performance of English CR, which should be comparable with the CoNLL shared task systems. Second, English coreference projected to the target language was evaluated. It should quantify the effect of cross-lingual projection of coreference. Third, all projected coreference relations were transferred to the tectogrammatical layer and

Score	German							Russian						
	DevOff			DevAdd			EvalOff	DevOff			DevAdd			EvalOff
	R	P	F	R	P	F	F	R	P	F	R	P	F	F
MUC	19.0	50.0	27.6	15.7	59.6	24.9	–	16.7	64.3	26.5	23.8	57.5	33.7	–
B^3	13.1	56.1	21.2	11.1	57.6	18.6	–	11.2	71.3	19.3	18.2	56.6	27.5	–
CEAF-e	21.2	27.2	23.8	16.2	44.3	23.7	–	22.1	34.1	26.8	26.9	46.8	34.2	–
CoNLL			**24.2**			**22.4**	**29.4**			**24.2**			**31.8**	**30.9**

Table 4: Evaluation of the resolvers expressed in terms of Precision, Recall and F-score of some popular coreference measures.

back to the surface. This should find the price we pay for conducting coreference resolution at the tectogrammatical layer. Finally, we compare these figures with the final scores presented in Section 5 to see a penalty for modeling coreference.

The experiment was undergone on the DevAdd dataset (see Section 5), annotated with coreference in German, Russian and English. The English part was used to evaluate after the first stage whereas the German and Russian parts for the rest. Performance was measured by CoNLL score.

Figure 2 illustrates how the score declines as the system proceeds over its stages (from left to right). The system for English evaluated after the first stage falls behind the state-of-the-art CR systems by more than 10 points. This can be attributed to a 33-times smaller test set as well as to gentle differences in annotation guidelines. Cross-lingual projection seems to be the bottleneck of the proposed approach. The performance drops by almost 10 points in Russian, even more in German. This could be partially rectified by using better alignment techniques. The loss incurred by operating at the tectogrammatical layer is larger for Russian. It can be attributed to the parsing issues observed on Russian (see Section 3.3). On the other hand, modeling projected coreference by machine learning harms a lot more for German. The models are fit using almost the same feature sets for both languages. Therefore, if the drop is not a consequence of the only difference in features, i.e. word embeddings for German set, it probably results from a different extent of expressive power of the feature set for the two languages. However, this must be taken with a grain of salt as we inferred it without searching for any empirical evidence.

Overall, while our projection-based resolver for Russian is able to preserve 66% of the quality achieved by the English resolver, it is only 46% for German.

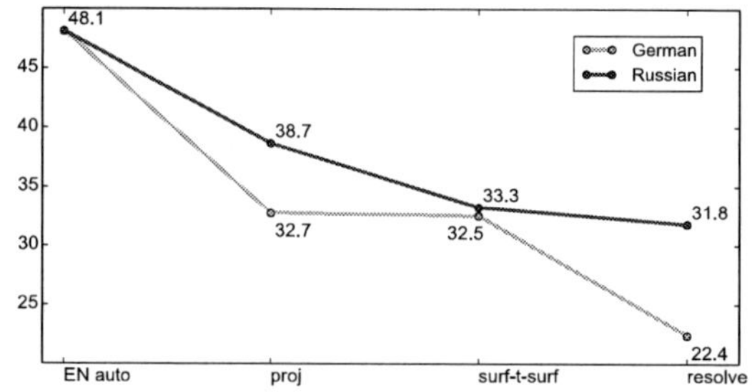

Figure 2: Performance decrease over the projection stages. Measured by CoNLL score.

7 Conclusion

We introduced a system for coreference resolution via projection for German and Russian. The system does not exploit any manually annotated data in these languages. Instead, it projects the automatic annotation of coreference from English to these languages through a parallel corpus. The resolution system operates on the level of deep syntax and takes advantage of specialized models for individual mention types. It seems to be more suitable for Russian as it is able to achieve 66% of the English resolver's quality, while it is less than 50% in German, both measured by CoNLL score. We submitted the system to the closed track of the CORBON 2017 Shared task.

Acknowledgments

This project has been funded by the Czech Science Foundation grant GA-16-05394S and the GAUK grant 338915. This work has been also supported and has been using language resources developed and/or stored and/or distributed by the LINDAT/CLARIN project No. LM2015071 of the

Ministry of Education, Youth and Sports of the Czech Republic.

We also gratefully thank to Katja Lapshinova-Koltunski from Saarland University, who helped us with annotation of German texts.

References

Mariana S. C. Almeida, Cláudia Pinto, Helena Figueira, Pedro Mendes, and André F. T. Martins. 2015. Aligning Opinions: Cross-Lingual Opinion Mining with Dependencies. In *Proceedings of the 53rd Annual Meeting of the Association for Computational Linguistics and the 7th International Joint Conference on Natural Language Processing of the Asian Federation of Natural Language Processing, ACL 2015, Volume 1: Long Papers*, pages 408–418, Stroudsburg, PA, USA. The Association for Computer Linguistics.

Amit Bagga and Breck Baldwin. 1998. Algorithms for Scoring Coreference Chains. In *In The First International Conference on Language Resources and Evaluation Workshop on Linguistics Coreference*, pages 563–566.

Darina Benikova, Chris Biemann, and Marc Reznicek. 2014. NoSta-D Named Entity Annotation for German: Guidelines and Dataset. In *Proceedings of the Ninth International Conference on Language Resources and Evaluation (LREC'14)*, Reykjavik, Iceland. European Language Resources Association (ELRA).

Anders Björkelund, Bernd Bohnet, Love Hafdell, and Pierre Nugues. 2010. A High-performance Syntactic and Semantic Dependency Parser. In *Proceedings of the 23rd International Conference on Computational Linguistics: Demonstrations*, pages 33–36, Stroudsburg, PA, USA. Association for Computational Linguistics.

Igor Boguslavsky, Svetlana Grigorieva, Nikolai Grigoriev, Leonid Kreidlin, and Nadezhda Frid. 2000. Dependency Treebank for Russian: Concept, Tools, Types of Information. In *Proceedings of the 18th Conference on Computational Linguistics-Volume 2*, pages 987–991, Morristown, NJ, USA. Association for Computational Linguistics.

Bernd Bohnet and Joakim Nivre. 2012. A Transition-based System for Joint Part-of-speech Tagging and Labeled Non-projective Dependency Parsing. In *Proceedings of the 2012 Joint Conference on Empirical Methods in Natural Language Processing and Computational Natural Language Learning*, pages 1455–1465, Stroudsburg, PA, USA. Association for Computational Linguistics.

José G. C. de Souza and Constantin Orăsan. 2011. Can Projected Chains in Parallel Corpora Help Coreference Resolution? In *Proceedings of the 8th International Conference on Anaphora Processing and Applications*, pages 59–69, Berlin, Heidelberg. Springer-Verlag.

Pascal Denis and Jason Baldridge. 2007. A Ranking Approach to Pronoun Resolution. In *Proceedings of the 20th International Joint Conference on Artifical Intelligence*, pages 1588–1593, San Francisco, CA, USA. Morgan Kaufmann Publishers Inc.

Greg Durrett and Dan Klein. 2014. A Joint Model for Entity Analysis: Coreference, Typing, and Linking. *TACL*, 2:477–490.

Yulia Grishina. 2017. CORBON 2017 Shared Task: Projection-Based Coreference Resolution. In *The 15th Conference of the European Chapter of the Association for Computational Linguistics, Proceedings of the Conference, Vol. 1 (Long Papers)*, Stroudsburg, PA, USA. Association for Computational Linguistics.

Rebecca Hwa, Philip Resnik, Amy Weinberg, Clara Cabezas, and Okan Kolak. 2005. Bootstrapping Parsers via Syntactic Projection Across Parallel Texts. *Natural Language Engineering*, 11(3):311–325.

Xiaoqiang Luo. 2005. On Coreference Resolution Performance Metrics. In *Proceedings of the Conference on Human Language Technology and Empirical Methods in Natural Language Processing*, pages 25–32, Stroudsburg, PA, USA. Association for Computational Linguistics.

André F. T. Martins. 2015. Transferring Coreference Resolvers with Posterior Regularization. In *Proceedings of the 53rd Annual Meeting of the Association for Computational Linguistics and the 7th International Joint Conference on Natural Language Processing of the Asian Federation of Natural Language Processing, ACL 2015, Volume 1: Long Papers*, pages 1427–1437, Stroudsburg, PA, USA. Association for Computational Linguistics.

Tomas Mikolov, Kai Chen, Greg Corrado, and Jeffrey Dean. 2013. Efficient Estimation of Word Representations in Vector Space. In *Proceedings of Workshop at ICLR*.

Valerie Mozharova and Natalia Loukachevitch. 2016. Two-stage Approach in Russian Named Entity Recognition. In *Proceedings of the International FRUCT Conference on Intelligence, Social Media and Web (ISMW FRUCT 2016)*, pages 43–48, Saint Petersburg.

Franz J. Och and Hermann Ney. 2000. Improved Statistical Alignment Models. In *Proceedings of the 38th Annual Meeting on Association for Computational Linguistics*, pages 440–447, Stroudsburg, PA, USA. Association for Computational Linguistics.

Maciej Ogrodniczuk. 2013. Translation- and Projection-Based Unsupervised Coreference Resolution for Polish. In *Language Processing and Intelligent Information Systems*, number 7912, pages 125–130, Berlin / Heidelberg. Springer.

Sebastian Padó and Mirella Lapata. 2009. Cross-lingual Annotation Projection of Semantic Roles. *Journal of Artificial Intelligence Research*, 36(1):307–340.

Martin Popel and Zdeněk Žabokrtský. 2010. TectoMT: Modular NLP Framework. In *Proceedings of the 7th International Conference on Advances in Natural Language Processing*, pages 293–304, Berlin, Heidelberg. Springer-Verlag.

Oana Postolache, Dan Cristea, and Constantin Orăsan. 2006. Transferring Coreference Chains through Word Alignment. In *Proceedings of the Fifth International Conference on Language Resources and Evaluation*, pages 889–892, Genoa, Italy. European Language Resources Association.

Sameer Pradhan, Alessandro Moschitti, Nianwen Xue, Olga Uryupina, and Yuchen Zhang. 2012. CoNLL-2012 Shared Task: Modeling Multilingual Unrestricted Coreference in OntoNotes. In *Joint Conference on Empirical Methods in Natural Language Processing and Computational Natural Language Learning - Proceedings of the Shared Task: Modeling Multilingual Unrestricted Coreference in OntoNotes, EMNLP-CoNLL 2012*, pages 1–40, Jeju, Korea. Association for Computational Linguistics.

Sameer Pradhan, Alessandro Moschitti, Nianwen Xue, Hwee Tou Ng, Anders Bjrkelund, Olga Uryupina, Yuchen Zhang, and Zhi Zhong. 2013. Towards Robust Linguistic Analysis using OntoNotes. In *Proceedings of the Seventeenth Conference on Computational Natural Language Learning*, pages 143–152, Sofia, Bulgaria. Association for Computational Linguistics.

Sameer Pradhan, Xiaoqiang Luo, Marta Recasens, Eduard Hovy, Vincent Ng, and Michael Strube. 2014. Scoring Coreference Partitions of Predicted Mentions: A Reference Implementation. In *Proceedings of the 52nd Annual Meeting of the Association for Computational Linguistics (Volume 2: Short Papers)*, pages 30–35, Baltimore, Maryland. Association for Computational Linguistics.

Altaf Rahman and Vincent Ng. 2012. Translation-based Projection for Multilingual Coreference Resolution. In *Proceedings of the 2012 Conference of the North American Chapter of the Association for Computational Linguistics: Human Language Technologies*, pages 968–977, Stroudsburg, PA, USA. Association for Computational Linguistics.

Helmut Schmid. 1995. Improvements In Part-of-Speech Tagging With an Application To German. In *In Proceedings of the ACL SIGDAT-Workshop*, pages 47–50, Stroudsburg, PA, USA. Association for Computational Linguistics.

Wolfgang Seeker and Jonas Kuhn. 2012. Making Ellipses Explicit in Dependency Conversion for a German Treebank. In *Proceedings of the Eight International Conference on Language Resources and Evaluation*, pages 3132–3139, Istanbul, Turkey. European Language Resources Association (ELRA).

Petr Sgall, Eva Hajičová, Jarmila Panevová, and Jacob Mey. 1986. *The meaning of the sentence in its semantic and pragmatic aspects*. Springer.

Milan Straka, Jan Hajič, and Jana Straková. 2016. UDPipe: Trainable Pipeline for Processing CoNLL-U Files Performing Tokenization, Morphological Analysis, POS Tagging and Parsing. In *Proceedings of the Tenth International Conference on Language Resources and Evaluation (LREC'16)*, pages 4290–4297, Paris, France. European Language Resources Association (ELRA).

Jana Straková, Milan Straka, and Jan Hajič. 2014. Open-Source Tools for Morphology, Lemmatization, POS Tagging and Named Entity Recognition. In *Proceedings of 52nd Annual Meeting of the Association for Computational Linguistics: System Demonstrations*, pages 13–18, Baltimore, Maryland. Association for Computational Linguistics.

Oscar Täckström, Dipanjan Das, Slav Petrov, Ryan T. McDonald, and Joakim Nivre. 2013. Token and Type Constraints for Cross-Lingual Part-of-Speech Tagging. *TACL*, 1:1–12.

Jörg Tiedemann. 2012. Parallel Data, Tools and Interfaces in OPUS. In *Proceedings of the Eight International Conference on Language Resources and Evaluation (LREC'12)*, pages 2214–2218, Paris, France. European Language Resources Association.

Marc Vilain, John Burger, John Aberdeen, Dennis Connolly, and Lynette Hirschman. 1995. A Model-theoretic Coreference Scoring Scheme. In *Proceedings of the 6th Conference on Message Understanding*, pages 45–52, Stroudsburg, PA, USA. Association for Computational Linguistics.

Daniel Zeman, Ondřej Dušek, David Mareček, Martin Popel, Loganathan Ramasamy, Jan Štěpánek, Zdeněk Žabokrtský, and Jan Hajič. 2014. HamleDT: Harmonized Multi-Language Dependency Treebank. *Language Resources and Evaluation*, 48(4):601–637.

Author Index

Amsili, Pascal, 24
Arregi, Olatz, 8
Arregi, Xabier, 8

Díaz de Ilarraza, Arantza, 8

Grishina, Yulia, 41, 51

Miculicich Werlen, Lesly, 30
Moosavi, Nafise Sadat, 1

Nedoluzhko, Anna, 56
Nitoń, Bartłomiej, 17
Novák, Michal, 56

Ogrodniczuk, Maciej, 17

Popescu-Belis, Andrei, 30

Seminck, Olga, 24
Soraluze, Ander, 8
Stede, Manfred, 41
Strube, Michael, 1

Žabokrtský, Zdeněk, 56

Association for Computational Linguistics
209 N. Eighth Street
Stroudsburg, Pennsylvania 18360

ISBN 978-1-5108-3863-5

CURRAN ASSOCIATES INC.
proceedings
.com